Jim Britt´s

Cracking the Rich Code²

Inspiring Stories, Insights and Strategies from Entrepreneurs Around the World

STAY IN TOUCH WITH JIM, KEVIN AND JOEL

For daily strategies and insights from top entrepreneurs, join us at

THE RICH CODE CLUB

<u>FREE</u> members site.

www.TheRichCodeClub.com

Co-authors from Around the World

Jim Britt

Kevin Harrington

Allie T. Mallad

Joel Sauceda

Mark Parsekian

Kim Erwin

Dr. Thomas S. Heemstra

Marty Daniel

Robert Proctor

Jeffrey K. Mack

David Volpe

Elaine Lien

Lisa McDonald

Phil R Mills

Hallie Bigliardi

Sonia Novick

Gary Goodspeed

Bennie McWilliams

JaNelle Garner

Mariana Light

Danny Kerridge

Ed Keener

Ryan Renick

DEDICATION

Entrepreneurs will change the world. They always have and they always will.

To the entrepreneurial spirit that lives within each of us.

Foreword by Kevin Harrington

You probably know me as one of the "Sharks" on the hit TV show Shark Tank, where I was an investor in many entrepreneurial ventures.

But my life and business wasn't always like that. I used to be your regular, everyday

guy patching cracked driveways to make money. I had hopes and dreams just like most, yet I worked around people who didn't support my dreams. But you know what? I not only found a way out, but I found a way to my dreams... and so can you.

Now, I wake up every morning excited about my day, and I surround with only the people I want in my life; entrepreneurs who really want something more than just getting by paycheck to paycheck.

Today we hear stories -- mostly from the mainstream media -- everyday about how bad things are, businesses are closing and jobs being lost, interest rates are on the rise, how the gap between rich and poor is growing and how you'll never make it on your own.

But here's what I know for sure. Entrepreneurs are going to change the world. We always have and we always will.

Forget the 1% vs the 99%. 100% of us entrepreneurs need answers. We need solutions. We need something more than what we're being told by those who don't have a clue. We need to start saying Yes! to opportunity and No! to all the noise.

The fact is that it's a new world and a new economy. The "proven" methods of doing business and investing that produced successful results, even two years ago, simply may not work anymore.

If you want to succeed (or even survive) in our new world, you need an entirely new set of skills and information.

You need to "reposition" yourself…often.

You need to revamp how you do business…often.

You need to change how you handle and invest your money…often.

Like any other situation, if you know WHAT to do and WHEN to do it, you'll not only be "safe"... you could easily skyrocket financially.

If you have the right knowledge for today, the right opportunities for today, the right strategies for today and most of all the right character and mindset for today, you can win — and you can win big!

What I've discovered in my over three-decade career as an entrepreneur, is that success in the face of financial adversity boils down to 3 things:

The right knowledge at the right time.

The right opportunities at the right time.

The right you... ALL the time.

The bottom line is this: you can no longer afford to rely on anyone else to navigate your financial future. You have to rely on your "self." The question is... do you have a "self" you can rely on? Unfortunately, when it comes to entrepreneurship and money, many people don't. They don't have the financial education, the mental toughness, the knowledge and the skills to build wealth... especially in an ever-changing marketplace. You need to get RE-educated. You need to REINVENT yourself for success in the new economy. You need to learn new strategies in the areas of business and career, finance and real estate that create wealth or at least financial freedom in today's new world. But that's not all...

Skills and strategies and all that profound new knowledge won't do you one bit of good if you don't have the CHARACTER, the HABITS and the MENTALITY it takes to get rich. If you have internal barriers, your road to success will be slow and full of pain and struggle. It's like driving with one foot on the gas and one foot on the brake and always wondering why you aren't getting anywhere. Your mind is working against you instead of for you.

I have seen business owners come to me with their business ready to go under — and have the next year be their best financial year ever. I've see others that had a business that should skyrocket, yet fail because they didn't have the mental toughness to go the distance. I have seen people stuck in dead-end, dreary jobs break out of their rut, get involved in a brand-new passion, and become wildly successful.

No matter what you do for a living...regardless of your education, level of business experience or current financial status…If you have a burning desire for financial change then you won't want to miss this rare opportunity to learn from the entrepreneurs within this book.

It will provide you with some of the same success strategies that Jim Britt and I have used personally and shared with tens of thousands of people who've had tremendous financial success…people just like you, who wanted to get out of the rat race and enjoy financial freedom.

In addition, you'll learn what others have done, mistakes they made and how you can avoid them. You'll discover strategies that could make your business into a major market leader. I always say "Just one good idea can change everything."

Success is predictable if you know what determines it. This book offers some valuable tips, knowledge, insights, skill sets, that will challenge you to leap beyond your current comfort level. If you want to strengthen your life, your business and your effectiveness overall, you'll discover a great friend in this book. You'll probably want to recommend it to all your entrepreneurial friends.

Although I haven't followed Jim Britt's career over the last 40 years, but I do know that he is recognized as one of the top thought leaders in the world, helping millions of people create prosperous lives. He has authored 13 books and multiple programs showing people how to understand their hidden abilities to do more, become more and enjoy more in every area of life. I also want to recognize Joel Sauceda, our online business partner. He is the brains behind the many online PR, Marketing, Branding and Lead Generation strategies each entrepreneur coauthor and reader of the book will benefit from.

The principles, concepts and ideas within this book are sometimes simple, but can be profound to a person who is ready for that perfect message at the right time and is willing to take action to change.

Maybe for one it's a chapter on leadership or mindset. For the next, it's a chapter on raising capital, or securing a business loan. Each chapter is like opening a surprise empowering gift.

The conclusion to me is an exciting one. You, me and every other human being are shaping our brains and bodies by our attitude, the decisions we make, the intentions we hold and the actions we take daily. Why is it exciting? Because we are in control of all these things and we can change as long as we have the intention, willingness and commitment to look inside, take charge of our lives and make the changes.

I want to congratulate Jim Britt for making this publication series available and for allowing me to write the foreword, a chapter in each book and be involved with the entrepreneurs within this book and series. I honor Jim and the coauthors within this book and the series for the lives they are changing.

As you enter these pages, do so slowly and with an open mind. Savor the wisdom you discover here, and then with interest and curiosity discover what rings true for you, and then take action toward the life you want.

So many people settle for less in life, but I can tell you from my experience that it doesn't have to be that way.

Be prepared…because your life and business is about to change!

Jim Britt & Kevin Harrington

As co-creators of this book series Jim Britt and Kevin Harrington have devoted their lives to helping others to live a more prosperous, fulfilled and happy life. Over the years they have influenced millions of lives through their coaching, mentoring, business strategies and leading by example. They are committed to never ending self-improvement and an inspiration to all they touch. They are both a true example that all things are possible. If you get a chance to work with Kevin and Jim or becoming a coauthor in a future Cracking the Rich Code book, jump at the chance!

Table of Contents

Jim Britt

Jim Britt is an internationally recognized leader in the field of peak performance and personal empowerment training. He is author of 13 best-selling books, including *Rings of Truth; The Power of Letting Go; Freedom; Unleashing Your Authentic Power; Do This. Get Rich-For Entrepreneurs; The Flaw in The Law of Attraction;* and *The Law of Realization,* to name a few. He is co-creator of 16 volume *"The Change"* book series for success coaches and speakers and co-creator of a collaborative book series for entrepreneurs *Cracking the Rich Code.*

Jim has presented seminars throughout the world sharing his success principles and life-enhancing realizations with thousands of audiences, totaling over 1,500,000 people from all walks of life.

Jim has served as a success counselor to over 300 corporations worldwide. He was recently named as one of the world's top 20 success coaches, top 50 speakers and presented with the best of the best award out of the top 100 contributors of all time to the direct selling industry.

Jim is more than aware of the challenges we all face in making adaptive changes for a sustainable future.

What ALL Wealthy People Have in Common

By Jim Britt

What's the secret to incredible financial success? The secret is, there is no <u>one</u> secret! The reality is there are many "secrets" that work together in combination with one another--- giving you the winning "combination" to succeed! Think of success like a giant vault at the bank with a thick steel door blocking it and a combination lock. Unless you have the right combination to that lock, it doesn't matter how much you beat on the door, how hard you work, how many lists you make or good intentions you have, because there is a combination you must know to unlock that door and get it to swing open so you can walk through to the other side. In this chapter I'll be sharing a couple of those success secrets with you… some straight-talk keys that make the difference between struggling your whole life in frustration or becoming wealthy.

Many years ago, I met a very wealthy person and I asked what inspired him to be wealthy? His answer really surprised me. "Money is a game and the man with the most notches on his belt wins." I was shocked! I was a young man at the time and having grown up without much I wanted to become rich. Yet after hearing this person's response, I looked deeper into his eyes and frankly, he didn't seem all that happy and the sense of lack of balance in his life was apparent. He was out of shape and had a look in his eyes of anxiety, loneliness and anger. I could tell that he had stepped on a lot of people to get to where he was.

How about you? Do you think that being financially wealthy takes putting yourself first and tramping over those that get in your way? Do you think that being wealthy means putting the lust for money ahead of everything else?

I've also met very wealthy people who give back to their community, have large circles of friends, and always seemed to be abundant in so many other ways.

In fact, a year or so ago I took a camera crew around the country and interview 11 self-made mega millionaires and one billionaire. The requirement was that they all had to have started with nothing. In other words, they didn't inherit their wealth. And all 12 made their money in different industries…internet marketing, traditional business, real estate, television, direct sales, social media, etc. If you asked any of these twelve individuals the same question, you'd likely get this sort of answer: "Wealth is simply a vehicle that magnify your deeper personality traits and mindset."

If you are a good person, access to resources, such as high achievers, it will only make you a better one. If your nature is negative, it will also magnify your unhealthy attributes on the downside, and you find yourself hanging around others that will support you in your negativity.

The following is what I have learned from my own experiences and the experiences of these 12 mega-millionaires and others I have associated myself with over the past 40 years.

Wealth is the ultimate power of leverage. Nothing is truer about becoming and deciding to become wealthy. It is a magnifying glass into your mindset.

I have tried to model myself after this philosophy, never forgetting that money is simply a means to achieving larger and greater things in life. After all, if the only reason you are pursuing buckets of money is to swim in it like uncle scrooge, you may find yourself the richest person in a very unhappy world.

Wouldn't it be nice if you could simply decide to become wealthy and you did?

Well, let me fill you in on a big secret…YOU CAN!

You already know the basics. You know that you should pay off your debt and start budgeting. You know that all you need to do is regularly invest money into your savings and let time do the work. Spend less, save more, build your investment portfolio…you've heard it time and time again. Then why aren't you on the way to becoming wealthy?

There are many reasons that people don't take action, even though they have the information. The reality is that so many people are just simply afraid to change. Fear takes a lot away from a person. They don't want to fail but when you buy into fear it will take you down that path.

Here's one key. For things to change for you financially, you have to make a change, otherwise you'll continue to keep producing the same results you've been producing. This may come as a shock to you, but most people really don't want to change. Just give them a beer, point them toward the sofa and give them the television remote. They will continue to complacently live out their lives.

Most people are much too busy earning a living to become financially free. They spend the majority of their time focused on what they *don't have* and what they *don't want*, on how to pay the bills, instead of focusing on what they *do have* and what they *do want* in their lives.

I know people, as I'm sure you do, that love having the drama of being up to their ears in debt. It's a balance beam that keeps excitement in their lives. It's a roller coaster ride that is thrilling but always drops them off at the same place time and time again. But at such a huge cost! What they don't realize is that they can't maintain their balance or thrill forever. At some point you have to decide where to get off…or you fall off.

I've often wondered, as I'm sure you have, why two people with the very same background and experience in the same type of business…one gains wealth, while the other barely survives? What determines the difference between someone who earns $50,000, $500,000 and someone who earns $5,000,000 a year? Is it their education, their experience, the amount of money they have already, or is it simply a lucky break?

One of the things I discovered in my 40-year career is that successful people do things in a different way. To put it yet another way…they do things that the majority of people are not willing to do. Most have been conditioned to believe that creating wealth is difficult, or that it's only for the lucky few. What do you believe?

Everyone wants greater financial success, but the statistics say that most will never have it. Get this…this is shocking! According to the U.S. social security administration the average retired couple has less than $7,000 in savings. At retirement 45% will depend on extra money from relatives for their survival. 30% depend on charity. 20% will still be working, and only 5% will be self-sustaining.

Wow! I don't know about you, but I find this unbelievable and even frightening!

I'm sure that people never believe, or even think, this would ever happen to them, but statistics say, it will! So, according to statistics, at age 65 there is a 95% chance you'll still be working for someone else and with no nest egg to retire or depending on relatives to survive. I don't think people plan for this to happen. No one in their right mind would make a plan like that. They simply don't have a plan for it *not* to happen. They convince themselves that "someday" they are going to be a success, to start their own business, to make a financial plan for their future, to have all they want in life…someday.

Someday...what an interesting concept. Think of all the things that were supposed to have happened by now…that someday that you may have convinced yourself was just around the corner. To most, that someday is where we've convinced ourselves we would be right now, if only we had more time, more talent, more education, more money, or maybe a better opportunity available.

How about you…is your level of financial success today where you thought it would be five years ago? Before going any further, I would urge you to stop right now and take a realistic look at your last five years. Have you truly made progress? Are the last five years what *you* wanted? Are you where you thought you'd be today? And, most importantly, do you have a solid plan for the next five?

You and I both know that there are no guarantees in life, but I'm going to suggest to you is what you've probably already concluded…for things to change in your life, you have to make a change. I want to help you to make the changes necessary to have all you want in life.

Too many people like to complain, but just don't want to make the effort. They don't have time. They'll do it next year. Let me tell you, you have to find time to get your financial situation in order if you want to gain wealth. Time is costing you money. The more time you spend trying to pay off credit cards, the more you pay the credit card company and contribute to their wealth.

I'm not saying to ignore your financial obligations. What I'm saying is that paying off your credit cards, although a good place to start, will not bring you wealth. Why? Because after you pay them off you are still left with the mentality that charged them to the max in the first place.

Don't let denial, fear, laziness, procrastination or a need for drama get in the way of your wealth plan. You *can* have all the money you want. It just takes learning and developing the traits that rich people use, and some time to make it happen. The pathway to wealth is something you can absolutely choose to take.

To become wealthy, you will need some vital traits. Let me offer you a few.

First is a firm decision to become wealthy. Wealthy people you'll find make solid decisions and commit to seeing them through. Those who are not financially successful put off decisions or mess around with their decision once it is made.

The first step in becoming wealthy, whatever wealth means to you, is making the decision to become wealthy…one that doesn't allow for anything less. Mediocrity is not an option to the wealthy. A decision creates a mindset, and a mindset makes you as mechanical and predictable as a calculator. Hit this number and it appears on the screen. Better yet decide on a number and it appears in your bank account. It's really surprising though how many people don't like to make decisions. They do all sorts of things to keep the moment of decision at arms-length including:

Gathering more data. Getting ready to get going…as soon as…Talking to more people. Getting other's opinions. Not thinking about the decision. Fretting over who the decision might offend.

Worrying about the resources needed to pull off the decision. Or hoping they'll just get lucky and make the money they need without making a decision, etc. All excuses for not making the decision.

The real problem is that most are stuck in a comfort zone and making a decision would possibly mean having to do something different that might be a bit painful. That's a decision we all face…the pain of staying stuck in our current situation or the pain of change. Most people would rather live with the "old you" for fear that becoming the "new you" would be too painful.

They say that the greatest instinct humans have is survival. I disagree. I believe it is staying the same. They stay the same for fear of the pain associated with changing.

Let's say a person makes a decision to be wealthy. What happens next when the old programs, the old habit patterns and mind chatter kicks in? "Wait a minute! What makes you think you have the talent to become wealthy?' "I've never done it before! Maybe I really can't become wealthy." "I don't have the expertise, time, money, etc. To become wealthy." And before long all the "self-talk" has pulled you off course and changed your decision (that you never really made in the first place) into something totally different from becoming wealthy. Sound familiar? We all do it to some degree.

Remember this: <u>every income level requires a different you</u>. You have to be willing to let go of the "old you" and embrace the challenge of becoming the "new you." And, if you want to learn, grow and change. You have to hang around people that challenge you to become better. If you want to become a million dollar a year earner, but yet you hang around and take input from people earning $60,000 a year, you'll likely to be right where they are financially. If you want to become a million dollar a year earner, *you have to make a decision to change*, and then you have to hang around million-dollar a year earners. Otherwise there will always be somebody offering you the wrong input and telling you how to run your life, making you feel insecure and doubtful.

I know people, as I'm sure you do, who go to work every day to a job that they hate. They hate what they earn and/or what they do, but they stay because they feel they have no other choice. They justify their position by calling it job security. But what they don't realize is that there is no security in a job! It's called *prolonged poverty* in my book!

It's like living in a place you hate but you're afraid to move because of your job.

Then you lose your job and can't afford to move, so you look for another insecure position that will keep you in the place you hate. *That's a sort of insanity, don't you think?*

What would I say to a person in that position? "*If you want to get better, you have to make better decisions, and you have to hang out with and take input from those who've done it.*" I would say "If you want to be rich, you have to stop working for someone else's goals and dreams and make a decision to start working for your own. You have to stop with the employee mentality and start thinking like wealthy people think."

So, the next time you catch yourself saying, "I have no choice," stop and ask yourself if that's really true. The more you make choices that move you in the direction of your objective, the faster you will arrive there. The faster you get input from someone that's in the position you want to be, the faster you'll get there.

Here's the key. It is your job to make the decision, one that doesn't allow for anything less. It's not your job to figure out how you will attain wealth until the decision is made. Your initial job is to make a firm decision. Up until the decision is made nothing happens…except, of course, the decision to stay where you are now. In reality not making a decision is a decision to leave everything status quo.

Let me ask you a question. Let's say that there are two components that make up 100% of your financial success. Those two components are "decision" and "opportunity, or financial vehicle." My question is this: what percentage do each play in your financial success? When I ask a group this question some say 50/50%. Some say 80/20 and others say 20/80. What do you think? Here's the answer. It's 100% decision and 0% vehicle. Because without a firm decision the vehicle doesn't matter in the least. Because without the decision there will be no success no matter what the vehicle. In fact, without the decision to become wealthy there is no reason to even search for the vehicle. That would be like shopping for something that you have no interest in having.

Rich people develop the skill of making the best decision possible with the best information possible in the timeliest manner possible. They are quick to decide and quick to take responsibility for their decisions - positive or negative.

The next trait all wealthy people have in common is that they are bold. Financially successful people have learned that action is vital. And often times that requires a level of boldness. They know that procrastination kills. They live with the reality of consequences and know there will always be uncertainty in decisions, but they boldly step forward and make the decision anyway.

No one can see all possible ramifications; no one can predict every contingency; no one can absolutely prevent failure. The wealth minded person knows that failure is not final, it's just one of those possible outcomes that happens on their way to success.

The real danger surrounding decision making is not "will I make the wrong decision?" But "did I make the best decision possible given the facts and circumstances?" Success minded individuals invest in learning what they need to make the correct decisions from those who have done what they want to do.

But, when it comes to investing in mentorship, so often I hear people say, "I can't afford it." "It costs too much." When in reality they can't afford not to," because it will cost you dearly if you don't. Wealthy people look at value not cost. What will the investment make them, or make of them, rather than what it will cost them?
The success minded, bold person, will always recover from poor decisions – they know that they'll learn and become wiser, while the meek minded will mess around and miss opportunities, saying "I don't have the time. I don't have the money. The timing is not right, etc." And when they finally do make a decision chances are their decision will have no momentum, no passion and no urgency.

If you wait for everything to be right before you decide, chances are you'll miss the opportunity all together.

The real question is, "what do you really want?" Are you like most everyone who is obsessed with success, with having more money, more things, and better futures for themselves and their family?

Are you intrigued by the top companies: success stories of rags to riches, who's the coolest, the hottest, the richest, the boldest? Are you just dreaming about success or standing on the sidelines observing other people's successes and wishing you had what they have? Do you justify why you aren't financially successful? Or are you bold enough to step out in the spotlight and take center stage before you have all the answers?

The real questions are: "Do you want to be rich?" "Do you want to retire wealthy?" "What would financial success look like to you?" Most people have never defined what financial success would be for them, and they've never made a decision to have it. And that's the only reason they don't have it! The most important question that you can ask yourself is, "have I defined what financial success means to me…or am I just working for someone else's success and letting them define my level of financial worth?" Or are you basing your future financial success on past experiences? How you answer that question can change your life!

Often times there is a feature in the investment section of some Sunday local newspapers. It's a success story column on people who've made it big financially in a respective business. You can also find those stories in magazines like Entrepreneur or Inc. You'll find stories of individuals who have carved out a niche for themselves in selected fields, lived a fulfilled life serving others with their skills and amassed quite a fortune while doing so. You'll always find one common trait in all the featured personalities. Not one of them. Not some of them. But this trait is in all of them! It's called a "wealth mindset." Despite the fact that they're from different backgrounds, all of them possess the same mindset when it comes to money. Wealthy people think differently. This is the infamous "money consciousness" that most of the motivational and personal development trainers speak of so often in their books and seminars.

This wealthy mindset basically means this:

Regardless of the physical condition that you may be currently in, as long as you see yourself bathing in financial abundance, your actions will maneuver, and circumstances will unfold in a way to create the wealth that you see yourself enjoying. If you possess the wealthy mindset, you will have the "Midas" touch when it comes to earning money. If you don't, you won't. That simple. The fortunate thing is, all of us possess the innate ability to fire up this wealthy mindset. But the key is letting go of the old you and holding true to the new you that you want to become. First is making the decision to be wealthy. Second is being bold. Next, is letting go of your limiting beliefs about money.

Some people frown at the mere mention of money. How many times have you heard people say something like this: "oh, I'm not doing this for the money" or "money isn't everything." Well, they're not wrong. Money isn't everything. The fact is that money in itself has no value. It's the things that money can buy when in circulation that makes it so valuable. Money can buy material possessions personal freedom, peace of mind, and we all deserve to have what we want.

At the same time, if you look from a different angle, once you've got enough money to be financially free, it can literally change what you do from laborious work to spending more precious moments with your family and friends as well as doing the things you love.

Money can also allow you to contribute to a charity and benefit the less privileged.
On the other end of the scale, some people tend to overvalue the importance of money so much so that they become slaves to it. They love money so much that they let this passion cause their downfall…we've all witnessed it.

In essence, if you never come to terms with what money can bring forth into your life, its real value, your uneasiness with the "idea" of money, it will limit your ability to attract more of it. To put it simply, just imagine this: Would you go into a car showroom if you've never had the intention to purchase a car? You may not want to buy it now, but the fact that you walked into the showroom implies that you appreciate the value of what a car brings. It can serve as a means of transportation for you and your family. And because of the perceived value you see to owning a car, you'll find the means and ways to get one. Having money is the same. Once you see its value and believe you can have it, you'll find the ways and means to getting it.

Remember, you can't create something that you're not in harmony with or that you haven't decided to have. Therefore, it becomes imperative that before you move onto other steps to really get this wealthy mindset concept. You should definitely have a conversation with yourself, or someone that can mentor you, to let go of the beliefs that's limiting you about money.

Having money means…finish the sentence…

What came up? Do you feel your answer will move you toward being wealthy?

Answer these questions:

> Why do you deserve to be wealthy?
>
> What do you believe about money?
>
> How did you come to believe this?
>
> Who taught you to believe that way?
>
> Were they wealthy?
>
> Who taught them?

The only way to change a belief is to challenge it. A belief is something that you have decided is true…it may not be at all. A belief is simply a decision that something is true. The good news is that you can change a belief simply by changing your decisions and letting go of the old you.

If you want to be wealthy, you have to first decide to be wealthy. Whatever being wealthy means to you. Next is to decide "why" you want to be wealthy. What's the payoff for wealth? Your "why" is the fuel that will take you where you want to go. It's the passion behind the decision.

Everyone has the right to be wealthy. YOU have the right to be wealthy….and yet, most allow a temporary lack of money to eat into our minds, literally confining them into the vicious cycle of mediocrity.

The bottom line is that people are poor because they have not yet decided to be wealthy. To put it another way…mediocre earners are mediocre earners because they have decided to be. They resonate with mediocrity.

So long as you make a conscious decision to become wealthy and have utmost faith that you can achieve it, and you let go of your outdated beliefs about money you will act accordingly to what you believe. Why not say "yes" to getting wealthy today! And say it with conviction.

Deciding to be wealthy only gets you started on the quest but what sustains you throughout the journey is the "why" you want to be wealthy and letting go of the mind chatter that pulls you back into your old habit patterns.

What is the reason that you want an extra $1 million in your bank account or you want to earn a million dollars a year? Why do you want to work your butt off, sacrificing your weekends to work a business or a job that only allows you to get by financially, when there is so much more available to you?

If you do not have a burning desire supporting your decision, and you don't let go of your old way of thinking and believing, you'll find your inspiration tapering off sooner and your decision fading into something totally different to being wealthy.

That's the trap that most everyone falls into.

Try this exercise. Take a piece of paper and scribble down all the reasons that you can think of why you want to be wealthy. Maybe you'd like to retire earlier and travel around the world? Or you want to quit your job and be a full-time parent? Write down as many why's as you can think of. Needless to say, the one that resonates with the deepest part of your heart should be written on an index card to remind you of the outcome you desire.

You'll also want to determine what wealth is to you. How much you want will inadvertently determine the action that you'll need to set forth to reach it.

Wealth can be whatever you say it is. For some it might mean 10 million in the bank. For others it might mean having enough residual income coming monthly to completely cover your overhead. For example, if it's $5,000 per month that you're looking for, working in your existing job and going for a raise in pay might suffice. However, if $100,000 per month is what you intend to achieve, other alternatives such as starting your own business, investing in properties or working on your "skills sets" to better serve the marketplace will probably be more effective. More importantly, knowing how much you want prepares your mind for the potential issues you may face to make that happen.

The challenge therefore becomes: How do you know how much you want?

Arbitrarily quoting a figure will probably do you more harm than good. If the amount you pull out of the sky is much higher than what you really want, your approach to acquire the wealth may not be in harmony with your "why" and you may end up burning yourself out. In the event that the amount is lesser than what you really want, then you'll find yourself re-adjusting your "why" which may not inspire you to keep going. Again your "what" your "why" and your "mindset" needs to be in harmony.

Determining how much you want doesn't have to be rocket science. You can do this by taking into consideration the objective for what you want the wealth for, your "why." and do an analysis of the costs necessary to sustain it. Let's say for example that your reason is to provide your family with a comfortable lifestyle which includes oversees travel for vacations twice a year along with being debt free. You can include the costs of paying off your debt, traveling overseas for holiday twice a year and your comfortable living expenses into your analysis.

A lot of people think having a wealthy mindset involves only constantly thinking about getting rich. That's not it at all. The most important element is to make the decision and after that not to obsess about how to do it. Take action and allow it to unfold. Play the "what if" game. Brainstorm possibilities. Be open to solutions. Expose your mind to possibilities…to new opportunities. Let go of your fears. Discuss with a qualified mentor or coach.

Suppose you want to get from point "A" to point "B." There's route 1, route 2, 3 all the way to infinity. When you believe that there's only one way to get there it limits your possibilities. When you are totally open to how to get there, the mind starts considering the many options and may prompt you to act on one of them that you haven't even thought of before. Along the way, your wealthy mindset may allow you to recognize different opportunities, encouraging you to change course and go through a totally different experience than originally planned.

I remember one entrepreneur I knew about that attained wealth in a totally different manner than expected. Initially, his plan was to market his own music compositions through conventional methods. But he instead stumbled upon online internet marketing and embarked on an unconventional route to becoming an internet millionaire. It was not an easy route as he had to juggle learning about the new internet marketing model of which he knew nothing about while still working a full-time job. But his burning desire to be rich got him through the hurdle to financial freedom.

Start to imagine yourself as already having wealth. Before you physically acquire the wealth that you've envisioned, you need to own it as if you already possess the amount of money that you desire! How would you feel right now if you were wealthy? What would you be doing differently? How would your life be different? How would your day unfold? Start to "own" the result of your wealth now! The subconscious mind is unable to differentiate between actual possession and mere visualization. So, by imagining that you already have it, you're encouraging your subconscious mind to seek ways to transform your imaginary feelings into the real thing.

I know many people refute this type of thinking as impractical. But if you think about it, isn't everything around us a true manifestation of someone else's imagination? Everything man made was in someone's imagination before it was created. And when they possessed the passion to create it the ways and means appeared. The Wright brothers imagined being able to fly and the reality is, we are now able to fly in an airplane from one country to another in a matter of hours. Thomas Edison imagined lighting the whole room using a single source and as a result, the light bulb was invented! Yes, it took a few tries, about 10,000, but eventually he created it.

Look around right now. If you are in a room, look at all the things in that room that made someone wealthy. Why not you? Take a walk outside and look around. How many things do you see that made some else wealthy? Why not you? It all started in someone's imagination. They owned it first in their mind before it became a reality. It's a fact that without the imagination of great visionaries, we would not be able to enjoy many things that we enjoy today. Radio, television, automobiles and thousands of other great inventions we would not enjoy today if not for someone first imagining it into existence. Vision comes first, then the answers!

You too possess the same capability to create, improve your own destiny by constructing it in your mind first. All improvement in your life begins in the improvement in your mental pictures. Change your mental pictures and you change the outcome of your life, like changing a movie in a DVD player.

So how do you build this imagination? Jack Nicklaus calls it "going to the movies" that's easy and fun to apply. He's known in the industry to have a very clear picture of how he should play the game before actually going into one. He visualizes an outcome before starting the game. He sees himself winning! In his own words, he states "i never hit a shot, not even in practice, without having a very sharp, in-focus picture of it in my mind first. He says, first I see the ball where I want it to fall, nice and white and sitting up high, easy to hit, on the green grass. Then the scene quickly changes, and i see the ball going there; its path, trajectory and shape, and even how it lands. Then there is a sort of fade out and the next scene shows me making the kind of swing that will turn the previous images into reality." You and I can do the same. For example, you can imagine receiving income checks when you open the mailbox every day. Or you can picture yourself receiving an award for being nominated the best entrepreneur in your country or having a best-selling book. Not only does it send the message to your subconscious, it serves as a great form of daily inspiration.

Okay, lets come in for a landing …

It is absolutely essential to have a crystal-clear picture of what you want to accomplish before you begin. If you want to attain wealth you must learn to operate with a sharply defined mental image of the outcome you want to attain.

Focus your attention on the spot where you want to land, not on where you are now, or on any misconceptions or shortcomings you may think you have. In other words, visualize your arrival and you'll develop a magnetic harmony with the ways and means required to get there. With a clear mental image, you'll attract the people and circumstances needed to get you where you want to go. Solutions will begin to appear, and obstacles will seem to disappear. Answers will come to you. People will show up to support you in your endeavor. Look at the end result as something that you are already prepared to do, you just haven't done it yet.

You have the potential, and the resources are available for you to have anything you want. The only thing missing is your firm, unshakable decision, the wealth mindset and letting go of your old way of thinking and believing.

Think about this. Your success is something that you have been preventing; it's not something you have to struggle to make happen. You can't force anything into existence. All you can do is step out of the way and let it unfold. The critical key is to not let fear, doubt, other people, or mind chatter push your success away.

You'll find the solutions taking you toward your goals will come to you in the most unexpected and sudden ways when you let go of the old you and embrace the new you.

You don't need the *perfect* plan first. What you need is a *perfectly* clear decision about your success and the right mindset, and the ideal way to get you there will materialize. You can't get all the answers up front before the decision is made, so don't waste your time trying.

The success formula doesn't involve getting everything neatly organized, with everything in its proper place and sequence and all the risks eliminated before you make the move. If you want that then get a 9-5 job. But realize that will never make you wealthy.

If you want to be a wealthy entrepreneur you have to sometimes shoot from the hip, going into new territory and charting the map as you go. Be willing to cope with confusion for a while and shape your plan as you go. Allow some disorder, and then create order out of it. If you get too detailed in the beginning, you'll find yourself worrying over potential problems and non-productive details, instead of what's really important, which is getting the job done. Get a target…point, then take action!

Your true greatness lies within your ability to decide what you want and commitment to having it, and then taking bold action to get it. Develop your mindset and then imagine it into existence.

You've heard the saying "think outside the box!" Here's my version… "don't ever get in the box!" The world you have perceived in the past is the world you now live in. The world you perceive now is the world you will create in the future. And the world you create is limited only by your imagination, your mindset and your ability to let go of the old you. Create your vision and then stand back and allow your conviction to decide the quality of your life and your degree of wealth!

Everyone has the right to be wealthy. You have the right to be wealthy. Yet, most allow a temporary lack of money to eat into their minds, literally confining them into the vicious cycle of mediocrity. The bottom line is that people are poor because they have not yet decided to be rich. So long as you manage a conscious decision to become wealthy and have the utmost faith that you can achieve it, you will act accordingly to what you believe. We all create our own reality, abundant or not. A person who believes that the universe is abundant, and they can attain whatever level of financial success they desire…and a person who believes that money only comes from working hard and will receive money only from hard work…are both right. Each will have many experiences to prove that their "belief" about abundance is a "fact."

The good news is though…you can change your belief and therefore change what you experience.

***

To contact Jim:
www.JimBritt.com
www.PowerOfLettingGo.com
www.CrackingTheRichCode.com
www.TheRichCodeClub.com
www.FaceBook.com/JimBrittOnline
www.LiveLifeAtLevelTen.com
www.linkedin.com/in/jim-britt

Kevin Harrington

Kevin Harrington is an original shark from the hit TV show *Shark Tank* and a successful entrepreneur for more than forty years. He's the co-founding board member of the Entrepreneurs' Organization and co-founder of the Electronic Retailing Association. He also invented the infomercial. He helped make "But wait... There's more!" part of our cultural history. He's one of the pioneers behind the *As Seen on TV* brand, has heard more than 50,000 pitches, and launched more than 500 products generating more than $5 Billion in global sales. Twenty of his companies have generated more than $100 million in revenue each. He's also the founder of the *Secrets of Closing the Sale Master Class* inspired by the Master of sales—Zig Ziglar. He's the author of several bestselling books including *Act Now: How I Turn Ideas into Million Dollar Products, Key Person of Influence,* and *Put a Shark in Your Tank.*

Becoming A KPI

By Kevin Harrington

The Key Person of Influence (KPI) in any given industry is the leader. It is the leader of the business world, the leader of automobile dealerships, the leader of selling hats—you name it. In other words, being the KPI means being the go-to person. The crazy thing? Anyone can be a Key Person of Influence. Any entrepreneur can be a KPI, a doctor, a salesperson, anyone. Just follow five steps and you will be well on your way. What comes with being a Key Person of Influence is value, ideally a massive amount of money, and being the leader in your field. The KPI is the person who comes up in conversations when it relates to a certain product, business, company, industry, or field. This is the person others seek out, the go-to person. Being the Key Person of Influence is how I got on *Shark Tank*.

Here's the story: I got a phone call from Mark Burnett's company. Mark Burnett is a television producer. He produced shows like *Survivor* and *The Voice*. His office called to set up an appointment. Mark was starting up a new show and wanted me to go out to Los Angeles to talk business. I was curious as to how Mark Burnett's company found me, and why they reached out for my services. They told me it was because I was a Key Person of Influence. I was all over the internet as a result of everything I was doing. It was 2008, and I had been in the business for 25 years. I had created huge brands. I helped build Tony Little. I helped build Jack Lalanne. I helped build Food Saver. We did the NuWave Oven. We worked with people like George Foreman and countless others. The problem was, everybody knew the brands, which was good for business, but did nothing for my personal brand. Consumers knew about the Food Saver, they knew about Tony Little, and they knew about Jack Lalanne, but not everyone knew I was the guy behind all of these people. Nobody knew me.

At that point, I made a conscious effort to build my brand. I wanted to become the go-to person so I could get the hot products and the phone calls. I helped build Tony Little's business, but everyone called him; they weren't calling me. What's wrong with that picture? Well, for one, I invested millions and millions of dollars of my own capital into Tony Little, and then he got all the phone calls. Shame on me for doing that, right? So, I decided to build my brand, and that's when I came out with my book, *Key Person of Influence*. I promoted myself by doing radio talk shows, TV shows, trade journals, speeches, etc. This is how I got on *Shark Tank*.

If I hadn't met Daniel Priestley, my book could have become *How to Become The Go-To Guy* because that's what I was looking to do, but Daniel very eloquently created this five-step system called the "Key Person of Influence." Realizing we were on to something, we co-authored and launched *Key Person of Influence*. Let's look now at the necessary steps to become a KPI.

Obtaining Customers

In 1984, I started a business of obtaining customers on TV. One evening, I was watching the Discovery Channel and suddenly the channel went dark for about six hours. I then called the cable company just in case there was a problem. They told me there wasn't a problem, that the Discovery Channel was an 18-hour network. That's when the light bulb went off. This was downtime. They put no value on those six down hours. Instead of showing something during this time, bars were put up on the screen. I started thinking about what I could put in place of that downtime, to sell something, obtain customers, and make money. I'm like the Rembrandt TV guy. I created and invented the whole concept of going to TV stations and buying huge blocks of remnant downtime. In all these years of me doing this, no one has challenged the idea that I was the person who did it, created it, and invented 30-minute infomercial blocks.

I was buying big blocks of time. Why? Because I wanted to obtain customers. How do you obtain customers? A lot of ways, but you ultimately have to get some form of media. How does it start? There are two metrics you have to look at when obtaining customers. What does it cost to obtain the customer? That is called the Cost Per Order (CPO). What is your Average Lifetime Revenue Value (ALRV), or Average Order Value (AOV)? The cost to obtain the customer obviously has to be less than the cost you are going to receive in income from the customer. The bottom line in obtaining customers: you have to set up a system. You have to set up testing. You have to set up as many sources for obtaining customers as possible. Even though I was in the TV business, I didn't just get customers through TV. Customers came through TV, radio, the internet, retail stores, international distribution, home shopping channels, etc. The first step is to make a laundry list of every possible resource for attracting these customers.

Today, some people who are into the digital space are basically just getting customers on the internet. Some of the areas I mentioned above have become very expensive. It's tougher to make money on TV. While we started on TV, the cost to get customers has become too high; so we now have made the switch to digital. When you talk about internet, there's many different ways to obtain customers, from Google AdWords to Facebook ads to social media, etc. You can also attain customers with public relations and influencers. You have to decide what works best with your product. The bottom line is, a lot of people do not realize they have to be sophisticated, from a business analysis standpoint, to set up a business. You need a marketing plan to obtain customers.

First, focus on two numbers: your Customer Acquisition Cost (CAT) and Average Order Value (AOV). Those numbers have to work. Customer service is crucial in the business world as well. A business can't have bad customer service and retain customers This is especially true in this day-and-age.

Raising Capital

I had a 50-million-dollar-a-year business, making $5 million a year in profit. Feeling confident, I met with seven banks to get some financing. I thought it was going to be easy because I had a very profitable business. Unfortunately, bank after bank after bank turned me down. I had great credit and all of that. The only asset I had was the business. Part of the problem was I didn't know how to approach the banks. I was a young entrepreneur in my twenties. I had no real credibility in the banking world; I was walking in and just showing my numbers from the year before.

So, what did I do to get the capital? Well, I ran into a mentor who was a former bank president, and he said, "Kevin, you went about it all wrong. I come from the banking business, and if you walked into my office and said, 'I need 5 million bucks,' I would have told you to turn around and get the hell out of my office. What do you have to do? You have to sell them on the future. What you did last year is well and good, but they are giving you money because they know that you are still going to be in business three years from now repaying their loans. You need projections. You need your forward business plan. You need your five-year master plan. You need to talk the talk and walk the walk, otherwise they aren't even interested."

I hired my mentor as a consultant to the company. I brought him in on the ground floor as part of my dream team. To make a long story short, we went back to re-pitch some of the same banks. We didn't get 5 million dollars, but we got a 3-million-dollar line of credit. It was all in how we talked to the banks. We had the same business, but it was all in the presentation. It's all in how you talk and how prepared you are. Raising capital is mental. It's in the pitch. It's in the relationships you build, etc.

One of the biggest challenges with any business is having enough capital to do the things you want to do. You have to have a successful business plan if you want to raise money. Here are the elements of a successful business plan.

(1) You need an executive summary (one page summarizing the whole plan). You need an industry overview, defining the problem you are solving and an overview of the market.

(2) You need a description of your product or the service. How does it serve as a solution?

(3) You need a competitive analysis. What/who is your competition?

(4) You need a sales and marketing plan.

(5) You need to identify your target customer and proof for your concept.

(6) What is your method of operations?

(7) Who's on your management team, your board of advisers, your dream team?

(8) What are your financial projections?

(9) You need to outline your risk analysis and appendix.

If you are going to raise capital, you don't just talk to an investor. I get people all the time that come to me saying they have an idea, and boom… it's on a napkin. They tell me that they just need $100K for 10 percent. I ask if they can send me their business plan. They then ask me what I mean when I say they need a 'business plan.' If they don't have one, that means I am going to end up giving them 100K and never see it again.

One of the most important parts of raising capital is coming up with a reasonable ask, and then explaining how the proceeds will be used. Many entrepreneurs don't understand this. For example, a guy came on *Shark Tank* saying he needed 150K for 10 percent of his company. I asked what he was going to use the 150K for?

His response was essentially this, "Well, I am going to use the money as a down payment for a piece of real estate where we are going to build a building, then launch the business."

"Okay, so you are going to build the building and then equip the building with furniture. Where is that money going to come from?" I asked. He said once he got the real estate, then they would figure out that batch of money at that time. I told him, "$150K dollars doesn't get you in business. $150K dollars gets you a piece of land. How are you going to build the business, generate revenue, and pay me back?" This guy told me he thought I would have more money for him after that. I said, "Well, no. You are not going to get the first batch of money based on the answers you are giving me."

Instead, he should have said he was going to lease a small office and start generating massive amounts of revenue with the money I gave them. Then, pay me back all of my money, plus a huge return on my investment, and then build it into a global business. That's what I wanted to hear. I want to know that people have a successful business plan, a successful marketing plan, and then I will talk about how to go about raising the capital, how to call on investors, and what the sweet spots are for the investors.

The bottom line on raising capital is, you can't just go build yourself a huge global business without thinking about how you're going to finance it. In the old days, I thought if I built a successful business, money was going to be easy. It's not, unless you know how to do it. There's an art to raising capital. Part of it involves making sure you are prepared and know how to pitch your business properly.

The Perfect Pitch

While the actual product or service you are trying to sell is a critical part of the process, it is just as important to sell the customer on yourself, your services, and your business. Even though I have made thousands upon thousands of pitches, have spoken to thousands of people, and have seen a great amount of success, I still pitch myself and my businesses. No matter who you are, or what you do, you have to be ready to drop the perfect pitch. It doesn't matter if you are going to make this perfect pitch in front of a crowd of thousands, or a crowd of one. To help with the concept of a perfect pitch, I have created a 10-step system.

Before you can start perfecting the perfect pitch, you have to ask yourself a couple of questions. What are you pitching? In other words, what product, business, or service are you trying to sell? Next, what do you want to get out of this pitch? More customers? More sales? Nonetheless, these questions are for you to answer, and you need to answer them before devising your perfect pitch. The perfect pitch can be broken down into these 10 steps:

(1) The **Tease** is your hook; the period of time when you plant the seed. This is when you reveal a problem. You have to explain to your customers why you are giving the pitch. You also have to use showmanship, which sets the pace for the rest of the pitch. If your showmanship skills are demonstrated in the Tease portion of your pitch, then you will have your audience (or your customer) hooked from the very beginning.

(2) Next up is **Please**. In this part of the perfect pitch, you are telling your customer how your product or service can solve the problem you mapped out in the first step. Ideally, your product or service will solve this stated problem in the most efficient, elegant, and cost-effective way. You have to relay to your customer that your solution is the best solution, and it will solve the problem better than anything (or anyone) else. It is important to also show off your features and benefits, and to display the magical transformation that will take place.

(3) The third step to the perfect pitch is **Demonstration/Multi-functionality**. First, you have to ask yourself if you can demonstrate your product, your service and your value. This is the key to any successful pitch, and it brings multi-functionality to the forefront. It shows it off. Think of this step as an added value. Ideally, your service or product is multifunctional. If you can show this off to your customer, then you just brought bonus points to the table.

(4) But Wait There's More! is the fourth step, and it's not just for infomercials on TV. This is the step where you give more value to your product or service by showing and adding more to the pitch— maybe added bonus items or "buy 2 get 1 free if you act now" incentives. At this point, your customer should already be biting, but now is the time to really win them over. So, show them what else you have to offer.

(5) Testimonials are the fifth step to creating the perfect pitch. You are now using someone else to do the pitching. In other words, who says so besides you? This is the proof behind your business, product, or service. Testimonials can include consumers (actual users of the product or service), professionals (leaders in your industry), editorial (articles, experts, press, journals, trade publications, magazines, newspapers), etc. Testimonials can also feature celebrities. Celebrity testimonials can be very powerful for the simple fact that people love celebrities. Then there are documented testimonials, which can include clinical studies, labs tests, and science. Once again, this is one of the most important areas for creating the perfect pitch.

(6) Another important step is **Research and Competitive Analysis**. For this step, you should be asking yourself if you have done your research. If so, then this is the portion of the perfect pitch when you show off all of that information. This can include information on the industry, market and competitors. It can also be facts, figures, and statistics. This research should show off the fact that you, your company, and your product/service is unique.

(7) The seventh step is **Your Team.** In this step, you are bringing the credibility of your team and putting it right there on the metaphorical table. Who makes up your team? It could be advisers, management, directors, and strategic partners. Your team will help scale, open connections, add on the knowledge factor, and so much more.

(8) Why? is the eighth step. Why are you pitching? How will the person in front of you help? This step will change based on who you are actually pitching to. For example, if you are looking for funds, then this is a big section, and you need to incorporate many talking points.

(9) The ninth step is **Marketing Plan.** You have done your pitch and given out all your information. Now, how will you make everything happen? For instance, you need to know your marketing and distribution plan. As is the case throughout your entire pitch, it is essential that you show confidence. Sell whoever you are pitching on your product or service, and yourself as well. People invest in people all the time.

(10) The 10th and final step is **Seize**. You laid everything out, now ask! What are you trying to accomplish? Ask it! Being the final step, this is the time to present the final call to action.

Remember, each pitch will be different. Some pitches last for over an hour and others last only a few seconds or minutes. It just depends on how much time you are given or how much time you need. That is why you need to craft your pitches accordingly. Practice, practice, and more practice.

***

To contact Kevin:

www.KevinHarrington.tv

Allie T. Mallad

Allie T. Mallad is founder, chairman and CEO of three national franchise brands, Massage Green Spa, Red Effect Infrared Fitness and Stretch Smart Infrared Therapy Centers.

An Ernst & Young Entrepreneur of the Year award winner, Mallad made his mark in franchising as one of the fastest-growing Little Caesars™ franchisees in company history. Mallad personally built and led a team of over 2000 employees and became the world's largest franchisee with 159 locations in California.

Mallad parlayed his franchising success across 10 national brands including Golden Corral, Big O Tires, Arco AM/PM, Applebee's, Baskin-Robbins, Bruegger's Bagels, Mobil Oil, Chevron Oil, Ryder Truck and Jiffy Lube. Mallad amassed numerous prestigious industry awards and was named one of the Top 50 Franchisees in the US by Nation's Restaurant News Magazine.

Mallad founded his own company in 2008 and became a national franchisor for Massage Green Spa, which operates 65 locations across the US and has over 175 additional locations in development.

In 2017, Mallad launched a second major national franchise, Red Effect Infrared Fitness, a breakthrough boutique fitness brand disrupting the industry with infrared technology enhancing the health benefits of traditional fitness. Red Effect is positioned to be a global brand because of the worldwide popularity of infrared therapy. Red Effect has opened 21 locations in 18 months and has 246 franchise locations under development.

In 2018, Mallad founded and launched a third national franchise brand, Stretch Smart Infrared Therapy Centers, to extend the health and wellness success of his massage therapy and fitness franchise concepts.

Addicted to the End Result

Five Proven Rules for Extreme Performance

By Allie T. Mallad

Do you ever wonder why some people achieve extraordinary things while others get lost or buried in the competitive pack? Why do some make history while others just make ends meet?

Extensive studies into the most extraordinary people in history don't prove that those with the highest IQ or strongest legs are the ones that win the most. Nearly 70% of the world's billionaires are completely self-made, some from deeply disadvantaged backgrounds. In fact, many have suffered horrible "luck" along the way – from unfortunate disease to devastating market crashes.

Extraordinary super-achievers are known to surpass expectations at the highest levels multiple times, even in multiple industries.

They bounce back and forth between failure and success, overcoming incomprehensible setbacks and adversity only to rise again.

So what is the secret sauce that separates the legends from the losers?

For my entire life, this was a question I just couldn't let go.

Born to immigrant parents in extremely humble conditions, tragedy struck early when I lost my father before my first birthday. What seemed like a mountain too big for even the most prepared, my mother quite literally carried my siblings and me through the darkest times without losing her vision for a brighter future and her unshakable sense of family and dignity. To this day, my Mom is my hero.

Of course, there are many that had it much worse than me, and I'm certainly not looking for sympathy. But it gets back to the question…. Why do some rise and others stumble?

In my own case, how could a kid from a disadvantaged, immigrant neighborhood, raised by a single mom, and certainly not being the smartest, strongest, or luckiest…. GO ON to create <u>hundreds of millions of dollars</u> in business value?

Having studied the difference-maker for the most extraordinary people on the planet…. and dissecting why I've been able to **win** at the highest levels when all signs would have pointed to a different outcome…. I discovered the **one thing** that all ultra-successful people have.

It isn't stunning creativity. It isn't genius IQ levels…. Many history-makers flunked or cheated their way through school.

It isn't talent…. In fact, the vast majority of childhood prodigies end up rather average by the time they reach adulthood. It's not luck. It's not smarts. It's not size. It's not environment.

It is all about **MINDSET**.

One specific mindset, actually. The most successful people – the Picassos and LeBron James' and the Mark Zuckerberg's – have **one specific mindset** in common that has fueled their incredible results.

They are **ADDICTED TO THE END RESULT**.

That's right. **ADDICTED**.

Most of us think of an addiction as a really, really bad thing…. A negative connotation…. a demon that gets the best of us, leading to tragedy and pain. We know the opioid crisis is tearing apart families and communities. Gambling, alcohol, and even spending addictions have created tragic endings to lives and families and marriages.

But can addiction actually be a powerfully positive driving force?

Merriman-Webster defines an addiction as "strongly inclined or compelled to do, use, or indulge in something repeatedly."

By that definition, it need not be a negative thing at all. In fact, what if the same compulsion was channeled for good?

An addiction to kindness, or charity, or compassion?

Even more powerful how about an addiction to health, to freedom, to loved ones, to family?

You see, an addiction – **obsessively chasing something until you get it no matter what and doing whatever it takes** – can actually be harnessed and deployed to your advantage.

And that's what Serena Williams does on the tennis court.

And Warren Buffet does in business.

And what Martin Luther King did for social justice.

Simply put – to achieve legendary extreme performance in life, we must be ADDICTED TO THE END RESULT. It is that relentless persistence that wins. Grit. Tenacity. Determination. An unstoppable will. An insatiable hunger.

The good news – this can be deliberately developed.

You can build, grow, and manage your own addiction to the outcomes **you choose**.

And **choose** is the right word. We all have a choice. We can choose to be mediocre or we can choose to be a champion.

Having spent over 35 years achieving far beyond what others thought I could do, and having scientifically studied the mindsets of the most successful people in history, I am excited to share a **simple five-step process** that have been the backbone of my own journey, and the building blocks of the giants in all professions and walks of life.

And they **can absolutely** work for you.

It's been said that the most powerful weapon on earth is the human soul on fire. Translation – pouring your entire being into the outcomes you seek.

Let's explore how we can develop an addiction for good.

Rule #1:

Be The Hungriest Person in The Room

To win in this hyper-competitive world, there is one deep-rooted, primal instinct that cuts through the noise of the crowd and will make you different: **HUNGER**.

I have often said that if I'm in a room with 500 people with everything from homeless people to billionaires in that room, I **will always** be the hungriest person in the room. It's all in my mindset. When I didn't have one cent to my name, I was the hungriest person in the room. Just the same, when I was the wealthiest, I was again the hungriest person in the room.

Plain and simple, being the hungriest is that **you want it more than anyone else**. That you **must feed yourself with achievement** in order to survive, in order to subsist.

Yes, being the hungriest requires an attitude…. which I always also say that "attitude is the mother of skill"…. but it also requires the action to do whatever it takes, doing what others are unwilling or unable to do, **to win**.

As simple as it sounds, successful people are willing to do what unsuccessful people are not willing to do, and it all grounded first in that hunger.

When you think about hunger, you cannot help but think about the nations and people of Africa who have long struggled to overcome things like famine and inadequate food supply.

The continent of Africa has a quarter of the world's arable land, and yet it only produces 10% of the world's food, which is a major pain point in feeding the people of Africa. This is pure and true hunger in the most primal sense.

And yet local farmer communities in such countries as Zambia are rising up, taking on the challenge boldly of overcoming their hunger and feeding themselves as a nation.

When you are among the hungriest nations in the world, you do extraordinary things to feed yourself. Zambia was so "hungry for food" and "hungry for change" that they single-handedly took on the challenge to communicate and show to the world that investment in African agriculture is desperately needed. But even more impactful, they carved a clear message into their mission which was **we are willing to do whatever it takes to produce more to feed our hunger, and the world needs to invest more in agriculture in Africa.**

There is no better way to feel the hunger for success than when you envision an entire continent united in feeding itself to survive.

Rule #2:

Laser Focus on Your Targets

Once you have fanned the flames of your hunger, your next move toward achieving extreme performance is to **lock in on your targets**.

It's the easy one to say – only five words – LOCK IN ON YOUR TARGETS – and yet it can be the most difficult one to do.

You need to realize that you just can't do everything on your list.

You can't be all things to all people.

Yet targets stated as goals give oxygen to our dreams.

We experience the strongest emotional response when we make progress on our most difficult targets and goals. My own philosophy for myself and my inner circle is that you must be absolutely laser-focused on your goals and on your most important priorities each and every minute of every day.

There is no long term without a short term.

And yet, I also challenge myself and others to continuously set bold, ambitious goals that get you to your dreams.

At times, these goals will go against all odds.

These goals will always have a purpose – and I love that key word *purpose*. I go to sleep with a smile on my face and wake up with a purpose which energizes me to attack these goals vigorously every morning.

Often, goals are non-traditional, off the charts, beyond the imagination, alien-like.

That's another key term that applies here – **alien-like** – which means out-of-this-world, not normal, not status quo, differentiating, superhuman.

Elon Musk comes to mind as a powerful inspiration when we think of alien-like approach to *locking in on your targets*.

Besides being very intrigued by the research on colonizing space and alien life in general, there is a method to Musk's targets in running his business and actualizing his visions.

Musk has been known to set unprecedented targets and unreasonable deadlines.

Musk stretches the boundaries beyond the norm whether it's with the Tesla, solar power, commercialized space travel or global sustainability.

And in staying locked on achieving those targets, Musk has produced game-changers. Musk's laser-lock approach to targets, and his enormous ambition and drive, is simply stated in three very clear things:

Think big.

Start small.

Move fast.

When was the last time you thought big, laser-locked on a target, made it your mission to get started even with the smallest step and once you got some early momentum, moved fast?

Rule #3:

Educate, Motivate & Stimulate the Talent Around You

What would rather have: Pure talent? Or the ability to recognize talent?

It's a trick question…

Some even say that the ability to recognize talent is a talent unto itself!

To achieve extreme performance, you must educate, motivate and stimulate the loyal, committed warriors at your side.

Choose to surround yourself with the best, feed your performers, starve your underperformers. My own addiction to success is fueled by watching my own army, those around me and closest to me, succeed.

I know that when this happens, in turn it explodes our collective growth.

It is all about emboldening and empowering that inner circle, those that step up to take care of the present, so that you can take care of the future.

You want to duplicate yourself every opportunity you get. You want to teach others to do your job so you can expand your capacity and satisfy your addicted to that end result, so that you can free yourself up to take on the extremes, the ambitious challenges and the enormous opportunities in front of you.

It accelerates your own growth, how fast you scale, how much you can fulfill your mission.

When I was building the Little Caesars Pizza business in California from 2 locations to becoming the largest franchisee in the world at 159 locations, in a record time of 6 years, I practiced the philosophy of educating, motivating and stimulating my people every single day.

I learned and did every job myself and taught my team one by one to do the same.

At the high point, we had over 2000 in our emboldened army serving our Customers and expanding our brand in a very competitive market. Those 20-year olds around me held the success of my business in the palm of their hands! I made it my mission to educate at every conversation.

Even if you are a lone wolf aspiring to extreme performance, you are still going to find yourself in a position of educating –motivating – stimulating others to get to where you want to be on that extreme performance track.

I use every coaching opportunity with my team and my people to challenge them to:

extend their thoughts,

think five levels deep,

not be robotic in their actions,

and creative problem solvers.

Every interaction is to educate, stimulate and motivate.

I always coached with the mentality that chance favors the prepared mind. I wanted my inner circle to be prepared to take full advantage of opportunities, making me and saving me money in our businesses.

If they are not and instead correcting problems, then they are costing me money and not able to be opportunistic.

The bottom line here is that educating, stimulating and motivating, on a daily basis, when made an inbred part of the culture of how you do things, ultimately achieves extreme performance.

A few more points to share about empowering the rock star team you want around you: great people don't quit companies…….. they quit people. The true alien top performers value the relationship with leadership and is what matters most to them.

Elite, extreme performers have a special set of skills that allows them to see opportunities and execute on those opportunities that others do not. Elite, extreme performers have an eccentric approach to their business, and at times a dysfunctional, non-traditional approach. They ignore anything and everything that detracts them from their primary mission and goals.

Nurture these elite, extreme performers and your ability to scale will geometrically explode.

Rule #4:

Fiercely Pursue Your Plan to the Extreme Edge

Do you embrace **extreme challenges** that lead to **extreme performance?**

Do your actions match your ambition?

Do you seek to mimic and copy?

Or rather innovate and disrupt?

I always say that **SUCCESS LEAVES CLUES** and that there are 8 very things to ask yourself when you are pushing yourself out of your boundaries, taking off your blinders and **extending** yourself to learn, grow and improve == **AND ASPIRE TO EXTREME PERFORMANCE!**

Do you believe in yourself?

Are you willing to put the work in?

Are you coachable?

Do you operate in good fear?

Will you constantly measure improvement?

Will you do whatever it takes to succeed?

Do you seek to master the discipline required to extreme success?

Will you conquer the temptation to quit?

Achieving extreme performance requires a fierce focus to the end result in terms of out-working and out-lasting your competition.

Every single day. Multiple shifts. Get used to it.

Getting deep into trenches and staying there a while… as being a champion is not an overnight gig.

Being hands on: see it and do it for yourself.

Becoming a detail freak – no detail is above you – or below you.

Bouncing back quickly after adversity and setbacks.

Learning how to win and wanting more.

When I first desired to become a Little Caesars Franchisee and break into my first national chain, I defied the odds and challenged the company norms almost to the point where I was turned away as an aspiring entrepreneur. It was a clear struggle to persuade a boardroom of corporate executives that I was their logical choice to go out to California from Michigan and plant the flag for the burgeoning national pizza brand in a new market.

In the end, demonstrating to the board that I had a bold plan with site locations already pre-selected and leases negotiated, that I would follow coaching and training guidelines and that I would step up and be an ambassador of the company as we grew were the extreme edges that opened up my opportunity for extreme success. I went on to live up to my commitments and would ultimately and eventually earn the distinction of becoming the largest Little Caesars Franchisee in the world.

Rule #5:

Trust most in your own ability to produce

It happens to most of us at some point in our lives.

If we are addicted to success and freedom and take those risks inherent in achieving extreme performance, things can happen to alter your course!

Maybe it's a divorce.

A broken partnership.

A miscalculation.

A hurricane or some other calamity that derails you.

In the blink of an instant, or maybe even years in the making… abruptly, unexpectedly, in a big ugly surprise, YOU COULD LOSE EVERYTHING!

Such an event or such events like these only verify that in the mission to achieve extreme performance, and tap into that incredible addiction to success, you can count on one security and one only and it's not your accumulated assets……

And that is simply this rule….

The only real security you have is your **PERSONAL ABILITY TO PRODUCE**.

I have often told those around me that if everything I had was wiped out and I had to start over, I would be back to where I was, back and better than ever, within one year. Some may need a little more time, maybe 2 or 3 years, but invoking this fundamental principle that you could come all the way back…. driven by your PERSONAL ABILITY TO PRODUCE will be the clincher in your ability to get to extreme results and feed off your passion and addiction to the end result.

This mindset was set by such icons as Andrew Carnegie, one of the first billionaires in American history. Carnegie lived by the personal ability to produce mantra.

He often said: "YOU CAN TAKE AWAY MY FACTORIES, MY RAILROADS AND MY CAPITAL, BUTY LEAVE ME WITH MY TOP PEOPLE, AND I WILL HAVE IT ALL BACK IN SHORT ORDER."

In the pursuit of extreme performance, if you have a sound healthy relationship with money, a fierce intensity to produce income at will through my personal ability to produce and my confident foundation of hunger, laser-locked targets, and ability to educate-stimulate-motivate, I too will be back and better than ever in short order.

Closing Thoughts

The ancient Chinese philosopher Lao Tzu once said, "The journey of a thousand miles begins with a single step." In the next 48 hours - while these ideas are still fresh in your mind – put these five rules to work for you right away.

If you want to start small, lock those sights on something manageable and achievable. The five building blocks work just great for the little stuff.

Or if you're ready be extreme and go big, lock your sights on that big audacious target. The one big thing that's your calling, that you want to be remembered for.

Don't we owe it to our companies to be addicted?

Don't we owe it to our families?

And communities?

And eventually our legacy?

We have opportunity to focus our addiction to do great things.

Addiction to health.

Addiction to family.

Addiction to success.

Addiction to freedom.

Addicted…. To the end result.

***

To contact Allie:

954-559-2117

alliemallad1@gmail.com

Joel Sauceda

Joel Sauceda is a self-made entrepreneur who got his start in the direct marketing industry at the age of 19. Known as the "Dot Com Guy", Joel has broken multiple records in the Online marketing & Direct Sales industry and is responsible for multi-million dollars in revenues over the past 20 years.

Joel has launched and sustained numerous Online and off-line ventures in his 21year business career. Joel is Founder of VortexAlliance.com, his personal coaching & mentoring community and serves on the board of SVJMarketing.com and ROYOL Music and is a partner in Cracking the Rich Code with Jim Britt & Kevin Harrington.

Joel's been featured in numerous publications and has had the honor of meeting Prince William and Harry, and a host of famous athletes and celebrities worldwide.

Joel is the father of two talented children (Veronica 22, Joel 19).

Joel is a former Air Force Reservist and Texas Air National Guardsman and his second passion besides Internet marketing and business is supporting causes that benefit wounded warriors and their families. Joel is also an avid cyclist with a passion for health and wellness.

C Minus to "Dot Com" CEO

How I Found and Re-Discovered My Passion in Life.

By Joel Sauceda

"The Re-Birth of a Passion"

Have you ever heard a song, watched a movie, or caught a glimpse of something or someone that sent chills up and down your spine? Now, I'm not talking about the kind of chills you get when you hear cats fighting or receive a bad newsletter in the mail! I'm talking about the "good chills", and this "classification" of chills often arrive with goose bumps; and, if you're lucky, they're the type that forge memories in our mind that we never forget. These good memories change our lives because they remind us of who you are, what we love, and in my case, they've served as reminders that anything's possible!

Before I dive in, try to think of the times in your life when you got these "good chills." The times when you were 100% certain that something good was about to happen for you. Maybe you got "inside info" that the person you had a crush on felt the same, you received the letter of acceptance to the university you dreamed of attending, you heard the shout of "B-6" for that definitive BINGO, or perhaps you were searching for the right career and something or someone inspired you enough to set you on the right path?

If you can't think of a time this happened, it's time to re-discover that flame that's still there because these "chills" are not disposable; they are gifts to you and regardless of how challenging times are, by re-discovering your purpose in life these "chills of enthusiasm" are available to everyone who's open to receive them! The great news is they don't discriminate! Age, ethnicity, or even economic level are not a factor.

These moments have proven more valuable than any stock or 401K plan in my life; and for a good reason, as you will soon discover, as

I share my own cases of the "chills" spanning over 40 years of my life. I look forward to bringing these moments to life for you as I've discovered how to restore and improve the clarity of these memories each year, much like old movies are brought to life with vivid colors and sound.

The "Chills" Of My Life.

Much of my childhood's memories have become a blur as I've grown older. One of my favorite Jimmy Buffet songs, "A Pirate Looks at 40" left the dock a good 5 years ago as I approach the big 5-0. While most memories have converted from video to pictures in my mind, the "chills" remain in vivid color for instant replay on demand. These moments of awareness are as clear today as they were back in 1986, a time of my youth when I began to realize these feelings might bring value to me. I was right. These "instant replays" have brought comfort and awareness in my darkest times.

So welcome to a small chapter of my life, I hope you gain something from my experience. May the "good chills" race up your spine and serve as a reminder that you are indeed special!

Life on the Air Force base.

My story begins on Dyess Air Force base, in Abilene Texas, where my father was stationed as an NCO (non-commissioned officer). It was there, in the fall of 1983, where I experienced my first "Chills of Enthusiasm". No, these chills did not involve a crush on a girl or a BMX bike that I so longed for; but rather, they involved a cheesy 80's movie about young people "conquering" the world with technology (Real Genius).

The rivalry, the drama, and to add to the memory the famed Tears for Fears song "Everybody Wants to Rule the World", played somewhere in the movie. That movie was responsible for many daydreams where I imagined owning one of the powerful computers these kids were hacking on. I was a technology junky early on in life, however the closest thing I had to a computer was a calculator watch that was missing a few buttons. And how can I forget my cherished "Speak & Spell" toy computer which displayed the recommended ages that were clearly below my age group. Adding insult to injury the Texas Instruments calculator my Dad would bring home from his Air Force job each day was off limits, so just dreaming of what I saw in that movie would have to do for a time.

Yes, an 80's movie was a catalyst for the technology field that's been a major part of my life today; and yes again, that movie and THAT song gives me "chills of inspiration" even to this day! Even though I knew absolutely nothing about real computers at the time, do we ever really know anything or everything we become passionate about in life? Curious enthusiasm for the computer led me to believe beyond a shadow of a doubt that I wanted one, and if I could ever get my hands on one, I'd never let it go. I got to the point where I would do everything it took to understand and learn how and why they were so powerful.

Texas Instruments to The Rescue Despite Being Crushed By The Apple!

A short time after watching that movie my future was presented to me once again in the form of a refurbished, discontinued Texas Instruments computer that my father brought home one evening. The $50 clearance price tag was a good enough deal for my father to pick it up from the Texas Instruments factory (which also resided in Abilene, Texas) and bring it home.

To this day I don't believe my father knew just how passionate I was about computers and what that "thrifty purchase" would mean to me. Furthermore, I'm not 100% sure this purchase was even meant for me; but my passion was so strong for this computer that nobody was going to own it but me. It was going to become my new best friend as I dove headfirst into the manual that accompanied this silver alien ship looking computer/keyboard. I marveled at how I could create moving pictures and even make up my own robot on screen that could ask questions and lead someone down a path who followed the blinking prompts that I had learned to create. Even the Archie comics, and the baseball in the back yard that I loved, took a backseat to this antiquated piece of technology. I later found out it was discontinued thanks to Mr. Steve Jobs company called Apple. They put that computer out of business, and I was passionately working and learning on technology that was obsolete. That would not stop me, something else would and it wasn't my love for the computer.

Time and Money Separated Me from My Love of All Things Tech.

Roll forward a couple of years with me if you would. The military soon moved our family to another base in a far off land called San Antonio, Texas. Allow me to set the stage for you once again. We lived in the basic housing that non-officer families were given (the other side of the tracks). Within these walls I grew up with penny pinching parents who were opposed to name-brand anything! If we wanted anything beyond the basics, we had to cut the grass and in return we'd receive a whopping $3. We also got the right to use Dad's lawn mower for my side grass cutting "ventures". As I type this, I can still hear my Mom scolding my brother and sister, and yes, me too! Some parents "scolded", my Mom's voice was SCALDING as she would lace her shouts with threats of belts to our butts from our Dad (I just got "bad chills"!). My parents did not believe in hand-outs and prohibited us from even accepting money from our Grand Parents! Grandma would always sneak it to me. Love you Grandma!

Back to my parents.

Mom was strong and wasn't the coddling type. I do not recall one time, as a child or teen, where she said she loved me. Mom grew up on the ranch and saying, "I Love You," as I later learned, was a sign of weakness. Feelings of excitement were also frowned upon in our house as well. Saying I'm excited or expressing it was like speaking a different language. I learned to suppress my excitement because my parents lived by the rule of "Never Get Your Hopes Up." This stuck with me for many years; looking back I know this was one of the causes for not allowing myself or others to be happy at many junctures in my life. And do I blame my parents? No. I've learned that every family has their issues and if my parents brought me up the way they were brought up, my life would have been even more challenging. Saying "I Love You" are words we say today. When I've been in the darkest times in my life my Mom and Dad have always been there, even if I was too stubborn to ask for their help. I Love you, Mom and Dad.

My parents provided us with our basic needs and occasionally a few "wants."

Mom was not a "phony" as she likes to say, and she was one hell of a multi-tasker! She could discipline, cook, clean, and smack us with a fly swatter when we had it coming! She would also deliver a dinner for the family just in time for my father's usual 5:30 arrival at home. This is where my LIFE listening skills took shape.

Dad would grace the table wearing a t-shirt, along with the other half of his Air Force uniform, and we would all hold hands singing sweet Jesus songs together! LOL (that's laughing out loud for you non-millennial). It was not like this in our home.

Now that I look back on it, these dinners were more like therapy sessions for my pops. Dad would spill his guts to Mom while devouring his dinner. We'd here all about his worries and challenges at work, and I'm not sure if my brother and sister internalized this but I was the ultimate "eavesdropper." Information was great data, good or bad, but in my parents' house we were only allowed to listen, and I did just that.

Fortunately for my Dad, Mom was a great listener. A woman of opinions, and after listening, she would air them uncensored! Yes, it was entertaining at times but looking back it was these dinner conversations that I took to heart and I found myself fearing adult money problems. I feared these more than my junior high school report cards. You see, my parents were not the type that micro-managed our schooling. If we had homework it was up to us to do it, and simply passing was more important than getting an "A". So, a "C" was the safety net I strived for because I hated school. I wanted the last 5 years of my schooling sentence to come to an end as soon as possible. Middle school and high school were not great memories for me.

I was embarrassed at the non-name brand shoes I had to wear. The fear of a fellow classmate pointing out something that I was wearing, that his mom donated to the base "Thrift Shop" where my Mom would sometimes find our clothes, was always there. I was always embarrassed and worried about what others would think of me if the tag on my blue jeans was not RED (remember the 501's?). I'd color the orange tag red or make KMART Non-Nike's into Nike's by using a razor blade to make the square logo into a SWOOSH. Looking back, it was insanity, but in those times, I worried about those things. And like father like son, I often worried about not being good enough or losing everything. Today I think about just how much I was like my Dad growing up, yet we rarely compared notes! What a resource we could have been to one another.

These experiences taught me to adapt to any situation, not because I was book smart but because in my mind those things were essential to survival in the school where I was forced to attend.

More Junior & High School Therapy.

Allow me to spend one more paragraph on the school subject.

I didn't dislike school, I HATED it. I thought the home comings and dances and "mums" (who the hell named them that!?) were bullshit. I remember classmates excited for the lunch bell. Why? The food sucked, and worst of all the entire seating "situation" was enough for me to skip lunch as often as I could so I didn't have to guess which lunch table clique I fit in with. And one more thing, my Mom worked outside the cafeteria as a hall monitor, imagine that!

So, I was a kid with a MULLET, a few Iron Maiden & Def Leppard t-shirts, bleached out jeans, a dangling grim reaper earring, and knock-off Nike's. Not much piqued my interest in school; well, with the exception of typing class where Mrs. Shultz taught me how to type 60 words per minute. Today I type faster than I speak! (How cool that Mrs. Shultz and I are friends on Facebook today, gotta' love technology!)

I viewed school as a prison sentence and was simply doing my time. I firmly believed that when I got out of school, I would find my way and it was NOT going to be college. I would someday be in business for myself. But, that's for another day another chapter.

So, what happened, why was I not involved in school? Why was I not on the baseball team and why did I not hang out with the "NERDS"? Why, the computer. The love of my life, the computer, had changed so much from the time of my first contact with that discontinued model. While my father did all he could to provide us with computers, I had forgotten how much I loved them. It would be several years beyond my eventual C MINUS graduation, in which I darted across the stage because I was now free, that we would re-engage.

Beyond High School.

College was something I was not interested in, especially after discovering the cost (Mom & Dad were not footing that bill!). Coming to the realization that the courses I would have to take all had the word PRE before them (Pre-Algebra etc), I was not going to waste any time in the school environment again.

So, rolling forward once again, it was 1999 when I caught the tail end of another movie that grabbed my attention. Another movie that featured that "CHILLING" song "Everybody Wants to Rule the World", "Pirates of Silicon Valley." As I type this, I'm grateful to that movie for reuniting me with my passion and a new passion I had discovered between the age 18 and 30, The Direct Sales Industry.

Direct Sales &Technology.

For the past 20 years I've dedicated my life to connecting these two passions. I experienced success in several Direct Sales industries leading up to 1999 when I saw "Pirates of Silicon Valley". Once again, I dove headfirst into discovering how I could marry the two. In 2001 I co-founded a tech-marketing company, and recently co-founded another tech company that makes marketing with technology easier for people from all walks of life and it is worldwide. This passion keeps me awake and motivates me day in and day out to improve and grow within these two life-changing industries. While there is so much more I could share, beyond one chapter, I'll leave that for another time.

For now, I must give thanks to the people I attribute the successes to and overcoming the many failures that these industries have graciously provided me!

First, I want to thank my Dad. A man of strong work ethic, integrity, and a love for his children and grandchildren that goes beyond anything I could ever understand. Next, I want to thank my Mom. She supported her husband through interactions and instilled a toughness in me that I'm so grateful for today.

And who else?

As Jimmy Buffet says in one of his songs, "I've learned from pirates and saints." I'll only thank the "saints" for now. I thank the late Dayle Maloney. I also thank David Manning, James Wiggins, Rick Lentini for teaching me so much and of course, the humble but wise Jim Britt, for the wisdom they've instilled in me to this day.

In closing, I've learned that it does not take a huge village to build a legacy; but rather true friends like Efrain Valdez, Andre Johnson "FNS" who've all contributed to a common vision each and every day. People who put others before their own wants in life and lead with their passion for what they do.

Last but not least, a huge shout out to my two amazing children who will someday carry my legacy on.

Until next time.

***

To contact Joel:

JoelSauceda.Com

CEO/ DOT COM Ventures

CEO/Founder VortexAlliance.Com

Mark Parsekian

Mark Parsekian has been a successful network marketer, business broker, consultant and entrepreneur for several decades, promoting natural science-based foods and health supplements. He has opened international markets, has built large domestic and international organizations and has served on company advisory boards.

A founding distributor and top earner in several companies, Mark is also co-founder of a Boston-based business brokering and consulting firm. He has helped companies and networkers (both skilled and neophytes) find opportunities supporting their purpose, needs and goals. Recognized for his business acumen and insight, Mark has written for well-respected publications where he shared his team-building approach to the development of successful sales organizations and his training techniques for building relationships.

As a motivational speaker, he stresses the importance of living with personal purpose, developing effective plans and taking effective actions. His openness about the "highs and lows" of his personal experiences have inspired many people to do what it takes to transform their current situation into the life they want and deserve.

Mark is a cold water swimmer and a member of the L Street Brownies and Runners of South Boston. He coached the team that built a 6-story human pyramid and 4-story human ladder wall *on roller skates* (listed in the 1988 ***Guinness Book of World Records***), demonstrating that the "impossible" is possible when people unite for a cause.

HOW I GOT TO BE RICH

Lessons Learned Along the Way

By Mark Parsekian

Happiness is the new Rich

Inner peace is the new Success

Health is the new Wealth

Kindness is the new Cool

--Anonymous

What is your definition of being RICH? For some people, it's simply having lots of money. For others, it's having fame or status. These days, many people define "rich" as enjoying a lifestyle of time freedom, health and happiness. How do YOU define "RICH"?

Whatever your answer is to that question, it is my intent to help you find ways to achieve your RICH life and be an inspiration to others.

By the end of my chapter, you will have learned what being RICH means to me and HOW I achieved the RICH lifestyle my family and I enjoy today. You will see that I am certainly not unique… My Story can easily be YOUR Story! By implementing key steps as expressed in these pages, you can be on your path to the RICH lifestyle you want and that you *deserve!*

MY PERSONAL STORY

As a teen, I was a good student and top athlete, very competitive and – outwardly -- seemed to have it all together. Deep inside, though, I felt very frustrated because I lacked the confidence, goals and sense of purpose that so many close friends seemed to have. I felt American greed, consumerism and corporate America were great evils in the world, and I wanted no part of it. I had great disdain for politics and politicians and felt our system of democracy was broken and owned by the highest bidder. To me, the love of money was America's new religion. I felt powerless and insignificant to affect change in the world because I lacked purpose, vision, and the skills to be a leader for change.

There were several influential people throughout my life. My mother, Berjig Javian and father, Harry Parsekian. My mother was always inspiring, positive and supportive. My dad was driven, tough and expected high standards for himself and his three boys. They both helped stretch my thinking and beliefs beyond my understanding, whether I liked it or not, and helped lay the foundation for who and what I would become.

My two high school track coaches, Thomas McGovern and Thomas Wittenhagen, taught me that until I felt I truly *deserved* to WIN -- seeing it, smelling it, tasting it before actually running a race -- I would not be victorious. In hindsight, this athletic training became a great metaphor in all areas of my life, especially in business! When I won the State Championship 1000-yard race that was "impossible," I made it into the newspapers, but my bigger take-away? The importance of *deserving* to be a winner!

FINDING PURPOSE

My freshman year at Northeastern University, my mother invited me to Harvard University, to hear a lecture on Buddhism: "Freedom and Influence: The Role of Religion in American Society." That afternoon changed my life completely because I learned:

- -All human beings have a mission in life that only they can fulfill, and *any* negative situation can be transformed into a benefit and something positive.
- -If you don't like something, don't complain. Get *involved* and change it *from the roots.* That is the only way to create lasting change in society.
- -We must become capable, trustworthy citizens within our communities and be humanistic millionaires for world peace.

I had never heard this kind of inspiration before and it touched a chord in my life and gave me purpose!

Following the lecture, I challenged all my beliefs about business, money and the American Dream and the responsibility I had for making America and the world a better place. I transferred from the school of Arts and Sciences to the Business School.

PLAN OF ACTION

Since that lecture, I began living with a strong sense of purpose. I wanted to become a millionaire AND make a positive impact. Not so easy to accomplish when you have no credit, little money and no experience. But I had *purpose* and *goals* and I began to visualize how to start. I had heard about wealth made from real estate (including my Dad's stories) and I wanted to create it for myself. Everyone thought I was crazy.

I wanted to buy a multi-family income property for three Reasons: To help single mothers and their kids have a safe place to live. To help pay for my college tuition. To prove that I could make good money AND help those in need. I had seen how my mother struggled to find housing for my brother Steve and me following her divorce from my father, so this need was very personal.

As serendipity would have it. I was walking in Cambridge one afternoon when I literally bumped into a real estate broker. He was in a suit and tie and I was a college kid wearing jeans, a t-shirt. We got to talking and I told him I wanted to buy a multi-family property in Cambridge. Surprisingly, he took me seriously, gave me his card and months later was the owner of a dilapidated four-family house near Harvard, BU and MIT. I benefited from historically high interest rates that had depressed real estate sales *and* from the good will of the property owner (who was willing to be my "bank"). I fixed up the four units and rented them to government housing Section 8 tenants who were mostly low income single mothers with children, fulfilling all three of my Reasons… including making a PROFIT!

I believed then – and I believe now -- that when you live with purpose, take effective action and are deserving of success, all things are possible!

STRECHING MY CAPACITY

After college, I managed an upscale gourmet natural food store in Cambridge, where I cultivated my passion for natural foods and developed my management skills and training expertise. Nevertheless, I was still unfulfilled. I wanted more – income *and* impact – so I kept reading, searching and developing myself. Little did I know that this job was perfect training for the greatest opportunities of my life!

I devoured many books on personal growth, money, wealth, and what makes people successful:

> *Think and Grow Rich* by Napoleon Hill

> *How to Win Friends and Influence People* by Dale Carnegie

> *Creative Visualization* by Shakti Gawain

> *Art of the Deal* by Donald Trump

These books (and many others) taught me about people, money, power, influence and attraction.

I digested what I read, incorporated it into my beliefs, and took daily action. (It is so important not only to intellectualize information, but to implement it!)

I could see my life transforming almost daily. Even though my lessons were often very challenging and painful, I remained purpose-driven and goal-focused.

MAKING THE IMPOSSIBLE POSSIBLE

At about this time, I was asked to lead a special group of over 200 men in an attempt to set a Guinness World Record. The concept was sponsored by a Buddhist World Peace organization to show what is possible when people unite together with a single purpose, like world peace. We were to make the seemingly "impossible" become possible.

Spectators who witnessed our successful performance on roller skates creating a 4-story moving human ladder wall and a 6-story human pyramid were awed... but not as much as those of us who accomplished these feats through teamwork and unshakable faith, courage and determination. We all challenged our own insecurities and beliefs while inspiring tens of thousands of people to work together to demonstrate that *anything is possible*. This activity thought me a powerful lesson: There is no time for failure or excuses in crucial moments. And when you want something badly enough, you make it happen. End of story!

As I began to see great changes unfolding in my life, I started to see that there are no "accidents" in life. Things came into my life for a reason; there was a cause-and-effect relationship to everything. I cultivated appreciation for everything in my life -- even the painful experiences -- because they helped me stretch my capacity the most.

IGNORANCE ON FIRE

On a beautiful Thanksgiving Day, my friend Ian Davies introduced me to a natural supplement networking company that marketed a blue-green algae superfood and encouraged me to try it. Little did I know that this company would change the path of my life forever! When the superfood soon cleared up my severe allergies, I excitedly shared the product with family and friends, (especially my athletic friends, because the product's amazing effects on workout recovery, focus and energy).

Everyone seem to want this product! Despite having no sales background or selling skill, I saw that network marketing's business model was simple: Find something that is impactful for you and share your story. That's how easy it is! I quickly built a large network and began earning more money than I had ever earned, *and* I was helping others feel better.

For the first time, I was purpose-driven and relationship-focused and having a huge impact on thousands of people. The money was a bonus!

At 28 and 29 years of age, Ian and I became the youngest top earners in the company, bringing in well over six figures in the early '90s. Simultaneously, we helped our friends and families (including my Mom) become top earners in the company. We were living the dream, changing thousands of people's lives, with no end in sight… until the bubble burst!

DIGGING OUT OF DEBT

Unfortunately, poor management decisions eroded the trust and belief in that company and sales plummeted. As I struggled to maintain the lifestyle I had become used to – without the income I was used to -- I accumulated tens of thousands in credit card debt at high interest, and I didn't have money to pay it off. Because of the stress, I suffered health symptoms so serious that my doctor said I could have a heart attack at any moment. It was only my lifelong athletic conditioning that saved my life, he told me.

The truth is I was never a good manager of money growing up. I was great at making it, but I was not skilled at keeping it. (This also seems to be a common ailment with network marketers today, so I now share with them what I learned the hard way: It doesn't matter how much you make if you have a hole in your pocket.)

From one of the lowest points in my life, I began rebuilding my health and confidence, one step at a time. I realized that achieving new business success was no different from enduring tough workouts or building a human pyramid on roller skates. I had to take everything that happened as a learning experience and KEEP MOVING AHEAD.

I entered a credit counseling agency to pay off my debt, negotiating much lower rates and avoiding bankruptcy.

A NEW BEGINNING

Coincidentally, I ran into a long-time high school friend, a CPA and a business valuation consultant whom I hadn't seen in years. When he asked what I was doing, I told him my current situation. Right then he offered me an opportunity to join in his small firm with a 50/50 commission-based performance. I was excited and very motivated. Within my first year, I sold four businesses and paid off my entire debt. Eventually, as I realized I was pretty skilled at negotiating business sales transactions and a "natural" at building bridges, I became one of the top sales brokers in one of the largest business brokering firms for main street and small businesses in the Boston area.

Not long afterward, two other top brokers and I left our previous company and started Northeast Business Partners, Inc. The skills I had developed in network marketing transferred seamlessly to business brokering and consulting, because it was all about building relationships. I realized that my talent for developing positive human relationships was the most valuable asset I had. Since the company's inception in 2003, we have sold millions of dollars' worth of businesses.

NO PAIN NO GAIN

In time, I began to miss the residual monthly income and lifestyle of network marketing. Then a seemingly "negative event" brought me back to it. While training for the Boston Marathon, I stepped in a pot hole and tore my meniscus. Forgoing surgery, I tried a new plant based nutritional supplement that my good friend Christian Drapeau co-developed. He co-founded a new company, marketing the world's first stem cell nutritional supplement. I felt this timing might be a "sign" and an answer to my prayers. Within two weeks, my chronic leg pain was gone and not long after my knee was back to normal and I was training like I had no injury.

I became a founding distributor in this company and introduced my good friend Ian Davies to the product, both of us deciding to share the business opportunity with others. We quickly became two of the top earners in the company, and I had over 100,000 distributors worldwide. I served on the company Advisory Board and was making more money than ever before. As a million-dollar earner, I traveled all over the world with my family, supporting and training distributors. But unfortunately, after 14 years of a great run, the company fell victim to poor top leadership. As it imploded, I decided to leave – as did many others -- to start another venture with a similar product.

Because of the successes and rich life my wife, Erin and son, Liam enjoy today, I have learned the importance of giving back. My two good friends, Larry J. Tish, Adam Gamble and I started a book fund for local community collage students in need. This has made a great impacted in the lives of many deserving individuals living with a purpose and taking action to make their communities and the world a better place.

Today, I leverage my time and skills in guiding people who are looking for home-based business opportunities and matching them to companies that best fit their needs. Every day I "practice what I preach": In business and in all of life, you must learn to become resilient, resourceful and flexible. A saying that always inspired me best during these times is *"Winter always turns into Spring."*

"This lifetime will never come again; it is precious and irreplaceable. To live without regret, we must have a concrete purpose, continually setting goals and challenges for ourselves. And we need to keep moving toward those specific targets steadily and tenaciously, one step at a time." – Dr. Daisaku Ikeda

LESSONS LEARNED

PURPOSE

Living with purpose gives meaning to our life. When you have a strong sense of purpose, any challenge or obstacle is fuel to further test your resolve and belief in what's important to you. Living with purpose strengthens your courage, confidence and perseverance.

GOALS

You need them! To succeed at anything important, you need to have short term, long term and lifetime goals. WRITE THEM DOWN and *visualize* them manifesting. (Studies have shown that writing down goals can increase their achievement by over 30%!) Having written goals is a good way to measure your success and to see how your Plan of Action is moving you toward reaching each goal.

THE PLAN

A goal without a Plan is just a pipe dream. Blue print the achievement of your goals with effective Action Plans containing "a sequence of steps that must be taken, or activities that must be performed well, for a strategy to succeed." Checking off each step of your Plan as you go will give you confidence in your ability to be successful.

DAILY ACTION

Action is what puts the life into your dream. It puts the plan into motion to manifest the goals. It is critical in any endeavor to make the daily causes to achieve the results you are looking for.

*"The most difficult thing is the decision to act.
The rest is merely tenacity."*

-- Amelia Earhart

AUTHENTIC LEADERSHIP

In business and in all of life, authenticity and sincerity build trust, inspire confidence and develop healthy relationships. The most impactful role models in my life were those who lived by example and who were not self-serving. They saw the talents in others that they didn't necessarily see in themselves. They were my parents, teachers, coaches, partners, friends, family and acquaintances who listened and who were available for support and guidance. Especially my wife, Erin and son Liam.

INTERNAL DIALOGUE

You can be your own biggest fan or your biggest detractor. It all depends on what you are telling yourself. Transform any negative thoughts into positive ones. The *positive* thoughts and *encouraging* words you say *to yourself* each day support your purpose, your plan and action and progress toward goals. Tell yourself: I am a magnet for success and will never be defeated!

DESERVING TO BE RICH

Almost everyone wants to be rich or successful in their endeavors, but many are not. Often this happens because, deep inside, they don't feel either capable, worthy, or deserving to be successful. The key, therefore, is to believe you deserve success and to know why it's important to your purpose. A good "why" to consider: When you are rich and successful, you can help others realize their potential to change their circumstances.

THERE IS NO FAILURE

Often it's the biggest challenges, the most painful experiences that spur our growth, to change us for the better. Really, there is no failure; it's only *feedback* that demonstrates what's working and what's not. The choices we make at pivotal points in life are what determine our success and happiness. I like to say, "I *failed* my way to success."

NEVER GIVE UP!

As a young athlete, I learned the importance of not giving up, no matter what! Breaking up big tasks or goals into smaller units of measure (your Plan of Action) makes goals more attainable.

Perseverance and unwavering focus on your purpose and goals are the keys to success and to being a winner. Stay the course!

ARE YOU RICH?

You are RICH when you learn constantly, utilize what you've learned and live a life of purpose. You are RICH when you contribute to effecting positive change in the world. You are RICH when you transform life's challenges into growth opportunities, never allowing "circumstances" to defeat you. You are RICH – no matter your current financial situation – when you focus on helping others. Reaching out to give someone else a "leg up" elevates you, them and the world!

***

To Contact Mark:
617-501-8486 cell
mparsekian@me.com
Mparglobal.com
Northeastpartners.com
www.turnthepagebookfund.org

Kim Erwin

Kim Erwin has found her niche by mastering the real estate market for the last 38 years as a real estate broker. She has coached over 1,000 real estate agents in her career and has a listing and sales volume of approximately $900m. Entrepreneurship goes hand-in-hand with her real estate business. Effectively "working the deal" is extremely complex because of the amount of individuals that are involved in the transaction, and managing it to a successful closing is her trademark. Determined to lead the way to help consumers understand the buying and selling process, she started a radio show called "Home $ense…Where Everyone Has a Voice in Real Estate." She is gifted with the ability to solve real estate problems while effectively communicating to those involved in the transaction while making it look effortless. In addition, she has written articles and authored books to help people maximize one of their largest financial assets, their home. Kim has received her MBA from Texas A&M University-Corpus Christi and Doctorate in Global Management and Leadership from California InterContinental University. Island life is for her and lives life to the fullest with a God-Driven Heart.

Mastering the Real Estate Niche

By Kim Erwin

There is power in every real estate transaction which equates to money. Mastering the transaction means knowing more than anyone else in your particular market. This is what buyers and sellers are looking for when they choose whom they want to hire. Growing your niche can happen much quicker than ever before thanks to increased technology and resources to work your market.

The first thing I always remember when identifying my niche market is what Gary Keller said in his book, *The One Thing: "Success is a result of narrowing your concentration to one thing."* I need to identify the one thing that stands between me and my goals, achieving extraordinary results in every transaction. This takes some soul-searching to clarify what my priorities are and my system for accountability.

I've learned that mastering my skill is more of a journey than an end and a worthwhile task to focus on. When I decided that I wanted to be the Waterfront Specialist in my real estate market, there was an extreme amount of time that I put into each one of the segment waterfront markets. Each market was different regarding the amount of waterfront that conveyed with the house, proximity to the Gulf of Mexico or open waters, such as bays. Other factors included whether the property resided in a mandatory homeowner's association, how many feet were available to build a deck or moor a boat, and whether the property was located in a Hurricane zone. There were so many more factors that went into becoming a master of my field while keeping within a 100-mile radius of where I lived.

This was a very daunting task and not very profitable starting out. I decided that I would list all properties, but my focus was on achieving the Waterfront Specialist status. Learning the markets took a long time, but I knew that progress was achieved by practicing performing comparable market analysis, listing, and selling the homes. Each plateau was a learning process, and I loved learning each market and working with the clients. I became an expert at practice.

As I was listing and selling non-waterfront properties, I realized that the variation of the markets was a subtle spice to take in my life. It was like mini breaks to refocus. I knew that my intentions alone couldn't transform me into the specialist I was seeking to be. The short-cuts became long-cuts and were not contributing to my job performance. My true blind spots were limiting myself to status quo compared to other realtors, not acknowledging the time and energy it was taking to achieve my goal.

I realized that I needed to build a strong personal brand online to open up new opportunities for me. I needed to build a team and go from a "me" to a "we" perspective. Another realization was the 80/20 Pareto's Principle of what was going to net me 80% of my business from 20% of my connections. It was easier to build the relationships with the 20% rather than the 80%. I realized that the short-term wins would eventually fill my long-term real estate goals. I definitely was prepared to do the sweat equity to achieve my measurable long-term goals.

The five areas I focused on to achieve mastery in my market was my mindset, accountability, clarity, resilience, and persistence. I knew I couldn't win all the listings, close on all of my written earnest money contracts, influence all of the buyers and sellers, and expect everyone to appreciate the knowledge and experience I brought to the workplace. This is where my vision expanded and compounded to "we" from "me." It was my most enlightening first step to building a team and having a business worth owning.

My mindset was aimed at working as a team and putting the vision of the team over my personal vision. I was interested in how they perceived my vision and what was realistic and achievable. My team became my inner circle to help me make decisions regarding marketing, social media, referral networks, advertising, etc. They helped open up my blind spots to problem listings and even difficult buyers. The shift of my mindset actually grew my team, which netted more sales and listing volume.

The systems and resources were already in place with the company that I work for. My team and I had to set up accountability processes to measure our goals and wins. This was where I discovered what worked for us and what didn't. That was not an easy achievement because real estate agents fall into the dogma of resisting change many times. I knew, through accountability, our vision and goals would compound quickly.

Clarity was one of the hardest areas for me personally to nail down. I knew that if I wasn't accountable to the team, I would be like my doggie, Precious—always chasing the shiny object but never quite satisfied with the outcome. During the negotiation process, there were times when the counter offers got lost in translation in the mind of my clients. I needed the clarity to reel them back in and confirm why they wanted to sell or the reasoning behind the purchase of a different home. Every buyer and seller are different. I owe my clients the fiduciary duty to assist them in making some of the biggest decisions of their lives. It is definitely not just about my team or myself, but also very much about my clients.

Resilience was definitely learned the hard way for me. I learned from failure—not getting this listing or losing that listing or having a transaction blow apart at closing. The culture of my team was that these were huge opportunities to learn and grow. Sometimes, it is worth firing an extremely difficult and energy draining client to open the pathway to ten clients that would truly appreciate our knowledge and expertise. The resilience that my team and I have achieved over the years comes from within and allows us to bounce back from the hardships of difficult clients and transactions.

It was through these stages that I found my team's unique path to success in real estate. We were intensely goal oriented with a clear identifiable vision to be the Waterfront Specialists in our area. It certainly increased our confidence and booted our motivation, while developing our competence over time. The shift in mindset brought about accomplishments that we never dreamed were possible. It was always satisfying to me to watch my team members grow and become leaders. It was healthy for our team to not be about one person but about everyone.

Another element that changed the mindset of our team was changing our culture to a completing vs a competing one. We focused on an abundant mindset, in that the listings were limitless and there were plenty of buyers. We think win-win and not win-lose. It lifted our morale and encouraged my team members to make each one better; it was a fun environment to list and sell properties. As we lead, my teammates also take the time and make the effort to understand the needs and wants of our buyers and sellers. Understanding these needs and wants makes it so much easier to "seal the deal" or close the transaction.

Some of the biggest challenges we see is the cost of time and quality of life issues with clients. One example is a retired couple who wanted to sell and be close to their grandchildren. They were missing out on watching them grow up and spending quality time with them. When an offer came in much lower than what they wanted, the couple still accepted the offer. I recommended that they counter, but it was the value of time. The money wasn't as important as lost time. Listening effectively to clients and customers is like money in the bank.

We have so much added-value services with our real estate niche. I wanted to be the go-to person if anyone needed recommendations or help. Sellers wanted to know a good landscaping company, the best painter, or the most honest maid who cleans excellently. Overtime, my value-added services were coordinating repairs for the sellers. The process was extremely difficult—getting bids and overseeing the repair work being done. Then, take this number by 20 every month, and sometimes I felt like I was a contractor and not a realtor. The positive side was that they were telling friends, family and neighbors about their positive experience with me; the referrals really started coming in.

As my real estate niche market increased, so did the volume of my sales and listings. The expertise of my team added to the mastery of our niche market. I would get calls from buyers around the world asking about waterfront, and they wanted comparable data immediately. Gaining the knowledge, combined with the experience, aided me in answering those questions immediately over the phone or internet. I saw the direct relationship of sowing the seeds of hard work and building experience to harvesting the fruits of our labor which equated to dollars and cents, plus a lot of pride of accomplishment.

There were many times that my team did so much work and the seller cancelled their listing and listed with another broker, and that home sold immediately. I realized that we couldn't keep score on the losses but rather keep our motives pure. There was recognition for what we'd done to try and sell the property, but it didn't work. I truly believe in the value of our services and what didn't work for one client has worked for 50 other clients, because we focused on always doing our best.

Another key ingredient to mastering my real estate niche was that my team had their daily focus on what needed to be done. They never lost sight of their long-term perspective and goals, but integrated the daily surprises in with them. There was also a shift in improvement in my team-to-team diversity vs team uniformity. We were not status quo anymore but developing the leader within each teammate. This shift offered an important opportunity for growth and expanding our market. The foundation was set and now it was time to grow exponentially and compound our effort.

It definitely wasn't easy to get to this spot. There was a lot of heartache, growing pains, questioning the sanity of each other, and not seeing failure as a doorway to great opportunity. As a team, we learned to place a high value on people and became "leader friendly." Our environment and culture shifted to one of higher standards, adding value back to clients and embracing and working together with other agents to close the deals. The best reward I've found is when other agents want to come and work for us. It truly is one of the highest compliments ever!

Achieving mastery in my real estate niche grew not only me, but my team. The testimonials of clients speak volumes for the successes we have achieved. I want to provide the best value-added services so that customers and clients want to hire us. The team knew that we had to give up old habits and dogma in order to move upward.

Through this team building process, I was able to compound the effort and replicate leaders so that I became the Waterfront Specialist for my market. It was not easy but extremely rewarding.

***

To contact Kim:

13957 Dasmarinas Dr.

Corpus Christi, TX 78418

(m) 361-688-9509

kimerwincc@gmail.com

Dr. Thomas S. Heemstra

Dr. Thomas S. Heemstra has Authored several published works:

STARQuest Character Education and Leadership Development Curriculum

Anthrax: A Deadly Shot in the Dark

The Change, Volume 7: The Words and the *Bees* of Bold Transformational Change!

Upcoming books:

The 7 Rights to … (Ethics)

I-25 Innovation Drive, the Creator's Road

Transformational Leadership Development…the Story

He is a former F-16 Fighter Squadron Commander with 15 combat missions in Iraq, a graduate of the U.S. Air Force Academy with a Doctorate degree in Strategic Leadership from Regent University. Tom is Founder of MACH 5 Leadership Solutions, an executive coaching and leadership consulting business. He is former Outstanding Adjunct Professor in Servant Leadership at the College of Mt. St. Joseph in Cincinnati; and is a Senior Associate for GiANT Worldwide.

He is Founder of *Creator's University*, a creative thinktank to help businesses with innovation and creativity; and teen students achieve their creative dreams. He is also Founder of the *The Sanctuary*, a not-for-profit retreat center designed for wounded leaders and injured soldiers returning home, and burnt-out pastors and missionaries. Tom is an International Airline Captain with over 20,000 flying hours. He lives near Knoxville Tennessee on gorgeous Norris Lake with his wife, Alise. And plays Pickleball at every opportunity.

Wealth of Connections' Conquer Circumstances, Chaos, and Corruption

By Thomas S. Heemstra

For "Cracking the Rich Code", 7 Rules apply:

Rule 1: Riches Abound when you discover your dreams, boldly pursue your destiny, and with your Connections persevere through challenges of corruption.

Rule 2: Caution: there is an enemy. Chaos seeks to kill, steal, and destroy those who can be devoured.

One who's been there offers his story.

He grew up in a small Midwest farm town "Salad Bowl City" working in the blueberry, onion fields, apple orchards, and celery farms but with no silver spoon in his mouth. He learned the value of hard work, and a great work ethic from wonderful parents that shaped his early years.

Dad's short perhaps unfulfilling stint in the Army drove Junior to an airshow when he was 6 years old, where the amazing Blue Angels performed. The stage was set.

While totally unpopular at school his parents enforced short haircuts, and white socks not just for athletics but with dress shoes, adding mockery to every day. Seeds from Rule 3 were planted then, to guide Junior for life's greater harvest.

Rule 3: "Dare to be different; and dare to make a difference." (Dad)

At age 10, his 6th grade teacher told him about the Air Force Academy and the dream was born: to become a fighter pilot like those Angels and attend this 4-year military college. Destiny seeds planted.

Water the dream and it grows right? But weathering trombone spit from the upperclassmen sitting behind him in the high school band was definitely 'over-the-top' and one of those hazards coming from students jealous of Junior's passion and goal clarity, or maybe frustrated by their own early personal failures in life. Maybe the horny saxophone play aggravated the trombonists too!

Rule 4: "Get over it. Spit happens"! (Dad)

So, he persevered; and overcame obstacles, mentored by incredible role models and teachers nurturing the dream.

Like most boys he had the 3 common deepest desires for a great destiny. His competitive soul was stirred by these early noble *battles to fight*, *a beauty to rescue*, plus the *adventure to win* for his warrior spirit. (Eldredge) These three always resonate deeply in the heart of those seeking the first rule of self-leadership, and the KEY Connection: to know themselves in order to lead themselves. (GiANT Worldwide) This was a journey of self-discovery, faith, and empowerment.

Failures, disappointments, and discouragement would test his real mettle. Adversity and accompanying adversaries would make the goals, riches, and rewards he pursued even harder to achieve. Although each time fresh new eyes, lessons learned, better perspective, helped achieve meaning, purpose, dreams, and propelled Junior toward his destiny to fly fast and formidable fighter aircraft, later proven when he instructed and inspired young airmen off-the-street, who had never flown jets to achieve their dreams as well.

On the horizon though as he got closer to his destiny, undetected, life's Strato-"corruptive" storm clouds were forming. Coincidentally, some of his friends were lost in aircraft accidents. These hit too close to home.

First fighter assignment Hahn Air Base Germany he found his new protégé, call sign Popeye. Early 20's young, small frame, lean but strong, and best of all exuberant. He walked briskly to his jet that day in March 1988. The early morning air was heavy with moisture. Not uncommon at Hahn, 60 miles west of Frankfurt, gorgeous setting near the Mosel River with manicured vineyards along rolling hillsides.

Popeye had an extra skip in his step, that confidence of accomplishment that brought him through the challenging Air Force

Academy as well. There he was an experienced and enthusiastic glider pilot, and now fired up, trained for this mission, one of the youngest of fighter pilots to strap on a $20Million dollar F-16, enroute to becoming a Top Gun.

Challenging to fly F-16s near the Berlin wall at the height of the Cold War. Helluva lot of responsibility, but up to the challenge; Popeye was checked out, and mission ready. Harnessing the 25,000-pound rocket with a thrust-to-weight ratio of greater than one: capable of going straight vertical, while accelerating, and capable of outdoing the human body with 9g's of gravity-squeezed acceleration. Typical roller coasters experience 2-3 g's. But Popeye could competently deploy this weapon system in air-to-air, and air-to-ground missions multiple times daily when needed.

Today was a single-ship mission but tweaked a little, because of so many crashes in Europe. Senior officers forced the mission be flown as a 2-ship. Sometimes single-seat airplane crashes with no witnesses made it difficult to determine what had gone wrong. And now General officers were under the gun to stop these accidents. "Fly it as a 2-ship" was their command directive.

Trouble was they gave no guidance how to do it. Typical uninformed bureaucrat-shoe clerks flying desks in an office. No problem. Junior as Flight Lead and mentor would fly behind Popeye through his target run first, then switch places. Squadron local leadership recommended this same setup to maximize Popeye's opportunity to learn--making decisions out front, 'simulating' that he was alone.

The sweet overwhelming smell of fresh JP4, jet fuel in the morning. Adrenalin-filled, Popeye did the routine walkaround inspection of his F-16 in the bomb-hardened tabvee shelter. Uneventful preflight start checklists completed. Taxi, all good. His Flight Lead followed Popeye then to appease the generals with this new 2-ship requirement.

Weather marginal today, very iffy but legal to go. Here at Hahn AB the worst weather of any U.S. Air Force Base in the world. Worse than Alaska, or Keflavik, Iceland. But trained, this was Popeye's time to prove himself as he lined up for takeoff. Cleared for takeoff, military-full power, now afterburner-5 giant kicks in the pants.

Rotate the accelerating rocket off planet earth, quickly raise the landing gear not to overspeed the gear, staying low below the weather and turning toward the first navigation point to get set up for the 500' altitude low-level at a blistering 480 knots.

Flight Lead with ultimate responsibility is 1 minute/8 miles behind. Popeye in front to maximize learning and training. Proceeding down track exactly on time to the Germeshein bridge, a well-known landmark on this low-level route Popeye had flown before. After turning, the weather ahead is looking worse, might have to 'route abort'. Sure enough, Popeye was scraping the ceiling above and no longer able to maintain legal cloud limits; and executed the route abort in a climbing turn, perhaps getting disoriented with glimpses of the ground; maybe looking over his shoulder for Flight Lead who is normally not there, except today for the General's insecurities.

Moments later, for the Flight Lead flying back to home base alone, everything raced through his mind, after a dreaded radio call from air traffic control announced a crash site had been found. Could it be possible Popeye is still alive? please God. What could have gone wrong? Time to shake it off, compartmentalize, and land safely. Remember weather's not great, and now a little stressed on approach to land.

Landing uneventfully, Junior was greeted by Popeye's Flight Commander, ironically nicknamed 'Deathwish' and the Squadron Commander in charge of 35 elite fighter pilots. Loss, sadness, and hugs of unrivaled camaraderie, amongst brothers who lived, trained, fought, and were prepared to die together if, or when, that day ever came. In a Cold War that just became colder, losing a brother, fellow warrior in peacetime, like so many others, gone too soon, not, no never forgotten.

As the only other American pilot in this particular German village besides Junior, under the adopt-a-bachelor program Popeye had become one of the family. Sensing the loss, their 4-year old daughter after that day would ask many times, "Where is Popeye?". "When is he coming over?" missing their frequent dinner guest? Months later they invited Popeye's parents over for dinner on their visit to Germany after his funeral in the States, hoping to retrace the last months of his life on foreign soil.

The official Air Force Accident Board retraced as much as possible what happened. Nothing explained the lack of radio calls from Popeye or what happened. But nothing would ever excuse the 1-star and 3-star General officers from later fabricating false statements in the accident board's official now-corrupt report to cover up the real issue.

Months later Junior would successfully rebut and correct the official records with help from honest Accident Board members who stood with integrity and friendship by Junior's side. Connections to Truth, honest friends, and their personal integrity overcame this challenge to a lifelong dream, that almost died too young, too.

Living the Dream, really?

Dreams do come true; harsh reality though, not always. There are dreamstealers, dreamkillers, distractions, and obstacles out there, challenges, circumstances, and people with their own agenda that don't support you and would blatantly rob you of your dreams. Many know this tragedy personally. Friends or family who don't support you, your dreams, and destiny, away from the rich and abundant life you would otherwise pursue. Fairness and justice are not guaranteed. There is no entitlement, to the riches we sometimes think we deserve, only hard work and a sometimes-treacherous process.

Furthermore, the villain is camouflaged in many life-disguises and distractions like fame, power, celebrity, success, riches, or alternatives like alcohol, sex, drugs and food. The enemy comes to "kill, steal and destroy", and sometimes not just figuratively. He is on the hunt to devour.

Success is best served when self-discovery is accomplished first. Know yourself to lead yourself, a critical connection to success and prosperity. Connections: Faith and family relationships are key to richness in life to weather the storms. Learn to fail forward. Fall back on those guiding principles and values. Most importantly, never give up.

Rule 5: We are created with a purpose, wonderfully crafted in the womb, and fully known by the Creator—His workmanship with gifts, talents, skills, abilities, dreams, calling-created for

good works which He prepared beforehand that we might accomplish them: our destiny.

Perspective, fresh eyes help persevere in destiny's passion. Priorities and purpose guide to the right path. For Junior, Faith was always before Family; and in his mind Family was before Air Force, especially now after the betrayal of senior leadership. Ironically, they also considered themselves family, the Air Force family. When the Air Force became uncertain, at least there was still real family though, right?

People would call them "Barbie and Ken". Her long blond hair, an attractive couple with incredible dreams, and everything going for them. Not so fast.

Divorce is an ugly thing, and these were two victims who tried to steer clear. "Barbie and Ken" vowed never to say the "D" word, until they became devoured by it.

Coaching two sports: basketball and volleyball for his oldest, junior high school daughter, for 2 years when other dads don't come to home games. Junior coached home, and away games, plus practices while flying for an international airline-his new transition career from the Air Force after Popeye's accident, plus flying F-16s again, part-time out-of-town for the military in the Air National Guard. That's how involved and dedicated he was to be in his two daughter's lives. Until one day it all came crashing down after deploying for 15 combat sorties in Iraq to patrol the no-fly zone, meanwhile a lurking predator back at home.

Vicious lawyer with a corrupt history and agenda for money, plus other things sought the destruction of the marriage, and family.

For Junior, fighting for fairness and for 50% shared parenting to protect his daughters was worth the battle against what experts observed and concluded was "severe parental alienation" targeting the father. He wanted and deserved that much time in his girl's lives, and that should not have been too much to ask for, or to expect. In the end he won joint custody on paper. However, the "family court" with a corrupt Judge who discriminated against fathers like many do, enjoyed this opportunity to exploit a successful airline pilot in the process and would not enforce shared parenting, or even scheduled visitation leaving the girls vulnerable. A failed "family court system" forced young pre-teens to make a choice that pre-teens were too young to make: choose mother or father; not both.

Heartbreak, loss, and betrayal. Of the marriage and family vows, of the court system, of the legal process. Taking a Dad out of his daughter's lives would threaten their futures. Wounded as a warrior against evil and corruption, the enemy tries to isolate, convince people of their failures, that no one has ever had it worse. Therefore, Junior's connections with Faith, family, friends, and flag were crucial to survival, and eventually to thrive again.

Junior's challenge: to persevere virtually from the bottom: living in a moldy basement with all his life belongings in one musty, dreary room. Junior now financially below basement from the $100,000+ court costs that enriched the corrupt so-called "Family Court system", and the pockets of Judges and lawyers who have no moral sense of family: meant refocusing, redefining, reframing purpose, and rediscovering passion-reconnecting with self, renewing Faith, holding fast to that connection.

Lesson learned: Compassion-a renewed perspective showing there are victims who need a victor to champion their cause when they can no longer fight. Because of that he remained committed to the ANG flying F-16s, instinctively knowing he was there for a calling, an enduring purpose beyond just having fun flying with the guys like a paid hobby that they all joked about.

Kill, steal and destroy. The corrupt enemy had killed a close friend and protégé, and now robbed him of his family. Was destruction next?

Looking at the Big Board F-16 flying schedule an intense young lieutenant came up to Junior, asking if he had heard about "The anthrax shot that is making people sick, killing some, and hearings are going on in Congress. The worst news: our Guard unit is slated to be given the shots soon before our next desert deployment, and we would be taking them early just to show how ready to go we were."

The anthrax vaccine program was a mandatory vaccination (AVIP) program designed under the Clinton Administration to give to all 2.5

million troops a 6-shot series, and 20+ over a career. The shot had never been long-term tested, was used in the Gulf War extensively, and was linked to Gulf War Illness. The shot was easily defeated in counter measures on the battlefield, was not proven effective, was being used for a purpose other than its original design which made it investigational or experimental requiring informed legal consent. The shot was therefore unsafe, untested, unproven, unnecessary, unethical, unlawful, and uncontrolled.

Corruption again: the former Chairman of the Joint Chiefs of Staff (Clinton's) Admiral Crowe was on the Board of Directors getting rich now that it was a mandatory shot for all 2.5 million troops. The vaccine prices shot up magically from $4 to triple that. This level of corruption forced senior military leaders to lie in testimony under oath about how many pilots refused the shot and were leaving their units.

Promoted to Squadron Commander (the dream of every young aspiring fighter pilot) after his devastating divorce, with 30-35 elite fighter pilots now working for him, Junior was going to inform them as his legal responsibility, so they could make their informed personal decisions, as required by law, rather than force them to take a deadly, dangerous, unproven shot.

Half the pilots decided to quit, hundreds nationwide; and he testified to the U.S. Congress twice as a Whistleblower about that loss of combat experience and national security hole, and the coercive program that cost his Squadron around 20 pilots at his base alone (nearly $200 Million in taxpayer investments). Six people had already died from the shot at the time, eventually a few dozen; after he also lost 2 friends, and squadron mates from Germany. Hundreds injured.

With America's 2-tiered so-called "justice system", Junior was then punished as a Whistleblower which is a violation of U.S. laws. The enemy now attacking his career passion, he was forced to resign as Squadron Commander, grounded-no longer allowed to fly the F-16, and forced to quit the military 8 years early, losing promotions and benefits.

Punishments continued 19 years later to this very day, stealing Junior's earned 20-year retirement pay after he filed 2 Inspector

General complaints, the first one not being answered by Secretary of Defense Cohen under the Clinton Administration, and the 2nd filed with President Bush. That one was forwarded to the Justice Department and stayed there for over 15 years without answer, to cover up for the corruption and crimes they committed: punishing a legal Whistleblower for legally protected speech to Congress, lying to Congress, and funding a fraudulent program and hoax on the American people and their military.

Margerite called Junior's hotel room one morning in Anywhere USA; and said "Thank you so much for saving my husband's life. You wrote the book: "Anthrax: A Deadly Shot in the Dark" and testified to Congress, right? My husband took 3 shots and was so sick, but he quit the military before taking a 4th one 6 months later and is getting better already."

Daring to make a difference made it worth it. (Thanks Dad.) One life saved.

How valuable was that?

Great connections conquer corruption. Father, family, friends, and mentors along the way; Faith-a heavenly Father, who loves beyond all comprehension, personal ethics, integrity, loyalty to an oath guided with these connections empowering one to know himself, to lead himself-his dreams, passion, purpose, calling and what gives life meaning.

Rule 6: Connections triumph over challenges, circumstances, chaos, and corruption where one can become more than a conqueror.

Gain perspective on the road to Prosperity. Setup a system of perpetual persistence and persevere to discover purpose, meaning, and richness in life. Continually write and re-write. Reframe your story with better perspective on the journey.

Then *"Right"* your story based on core values. Riches will be coming your way. Riches abound when you boldly pursue your destiny and persevere with your wealth of connections through challenges of corruption.

As you write, know that you can dare to be different. Courage.

Dare to make a difference. I know you will.

Rule 7: Start with Faith, Family, Friends, Flag; and Fortune will follow.

By now you probably know this was not just a story. Now you have read <u>my</u> story. That is "Cracking the Rich Code".

Dr. Tom Heemstra, Lt.Col. USAF Retired

CEO, MACH 5 Leadership Solutions, Executive Coaching & Consulting

***

Contact Tom via:

drtom@mach5ls.com   Cell (865) 585-0047, Please leave a voicemail message

Linked In: linkedin.com/in/dr-tom-heemstra-ltcol-ret-6246b8a

Facebook: https://facebook.com/tom.heemstra1

or Twitter: Tom Heemstra@HeemstraTom

TomHeemstraSuccess.com

References

Eldredge, John. "Wild at Heart", 2001.

GiANT Worldwide.

The Holy Bible.

Marty "Ocean Eagle" Daniel

After overcoming many life traumas and addiction, Marty was able to become a successful Real Estate Broker, Owner and Investor. A true rag to riches story that evolved through hard work, relationship building, trust, fearless risk taking, and a deep desire to give back what he has received. Marty lives in Elk Grove, Ca. and is raising his two children, Cade and Kennedy, who are both in high school.

Ever evolving, He is active in his spiritual journey with a host of friends developing around the globe as a result. If you are called to please feel free to reach out to Marty via Facebook at "Marty-Ocean Eagle Daniel". You can also find him by searching Marty Daniel Sacramento Real Estate on your favorite search engine.

A Warrior's Heart

By Marty Daniel

To say this is long overdue would have been an understatement had I not come to the understanding that everything happens when it is supposed to. I have been called to write for the last 6 months and then I get an email from Jim Britt's team saying they were looking for a co-author who is in real estate to contribute to this book. I have learned to not question the answers the Divine Spirit gives to me once I set the intention and send it out to the universe. I am always ready to say Yes these days even when I do not understand why I am supposed to take action in a certain direction. When I have faith and throw my heart into it, I am always amazed at the result. That is because I no longer look ahead nor have expectations as to what the result should look like……that's none of my business!

Being this is a book about entrepreneurialism I will focus my thoughts on my journey to financial freedom but first I would like to share a bit about me as I believe we connect with each by relating our experiences with one another. My childhood was less than what "Leave it to Beaver" or "The Brady Bunch" would have you believe a "normal" childhood should look like. I was born into an alcoholic and toxic family. I was taught by my father to never cry as Men do not cry. I remember having my first beer at age 5 and how it made me feel like an adult and cool. My father was a verbally and physically abusive man and his rage was something that stayed with me throughout my adult life. My brother was only 16 months older than me and an extremely troubled kid. He was on Ritalin by age 5 or 6 but that did not stop the emotional and physical abuse I suffered from him. I remember my mom in a loving way back then but I now know she was quite alcoholic at the time and later it would become more evident.

My childhood would soon become a war zone by age 6. My father's alcoholism, gambling and rage became worse and worse and soon the "Great Trauma" (there were many to come), that I now know guided my subconscious decision making, would happen. The first incident I can recall was a bright, sunny day and my dad came home in a rage accusing my mother of something and it ended up with him dragging her out of the house by her hair and down the driveway. He was calling her every name you can imagine and the fear and terror that came over me scared me stiff. Soon after when I was 7 years old my parents were separated, and my father came over on a Saturday morning and said he wanted to speak privately to my mother in the bedroom. I can't remember much about my childhood, but I can still remember the color of the carpet and smell in the house that morning. Once in the bedroom the next thing my brother and I hear are the horrific screams of my mother. My brother and I ran to the bedroom, opened the door and saw my mother's night gown torn in two on the floor. My mother was screaming and crying as my naked father was brutally beating and raping my mother. My mother was telling us to go and my father balled his fist and back handed her across the face breaking her jaw. He then got off of her and ran at my brother and I pushing us out the door and locking it. He went back and raped her more as I was standing at the door beating on it with my fist begging him to stop. My brother (8) ran next door to call the police. The next thing I remember is my dad, mother, brother, and I standing in the kitchen. My mom's jaw was black and blue and she was shaking like a leaf. My dad had this wild, crazy look in his eye and was telling us "we just didn't understand".

There was never any therapy or counseling after this as my mom had no money and had these two wild boys to raise on her own in the Bay Area of California. We became latch key kids at 7 and 8 years old as mom worked a lot and was also drinking a lot. I did not hear from nor see my dad for many years but later was forced to see him. I do not remember that reunion at all. My mom moved my brother and I from California to west Texas and I went to 4th grade in Roscoe, Tx. We moved into a wood shack with my grandparents on the corner of a cotton field next to the railroad tracks. The house would shake in the middle of the night when the trains would come by and My grandmother would feed the hobos who would jump off the train just before town and come to the back porch. Moving would become a major part of my life as my mom and future step dad went all over Texas chasing dreams that never amounted to anything. They were a good alcoholic team and we even owned a bar when I was a teenager. I went to 5 elementary schools in two states in 5 different cities, 3 Jr Highs and 3 High Schools as a result of their pipe dream chasing and the traumas from early childhood. My mom and step dad moved out of town a month before I graduated elementary school at the end of 6th grade leaving me with a friend of mine and his mother. After I guided my sophomore football team to a 10-0 season as their quarterback and got called up to varsity for the playoffs, my mom and step dad moved away again leaving me with my alcoholic Grandparents. When I would be sent to California in the summers to see my dad for two weeks, he would lock us in a van in a parking lot while he gambled and drank all night in card rooms. He would threaten us to stay in the van before he went inside. He would come out in a rage and drunk after losing all his money and I can't really describe the terror that man put into me. I was so terrified of him and I can still see the look in his eyes.

I think the only thing that saved me was my gifts athletically and I was a very warm-hearted kid. However, I started drinking at age 14 and my career as an alcoholic was set in motion. I never liked the taste of alcohol, but I loved the effect as I was able to numb all of the pain. I was a black out drinker from the start. I never wanted to just catch a buzz, I wanted oblivion every time I drank. I also abused many drugs through the age of 21 and afterward alcohol became my master. There was not much I did not try or use abusively honestly. I received a baseball scholarship somehow but had zero respect or appreciation for that gift. By my 3rd semester I was so far behind in my classes and doing so many drugs I walked away. I was in Houston at the time and moved across country to California to be near my dad because he had money and a business I could sponge off of. I could go on and on about my crazy life as an alcoholic and tell you a glorified version of what happened, but I think I have shared enough to attract those who can resonate with any part of my story. By age 25 I had totaled 4 vehicles, collected 3 DUI's and been in a Mexico jail. I could add to this list ad nauseum.

My brother who was in and out of jails and institutions chased his disease into the grave at age 22 as he lost his life in a drunk driving accident and we all got the call in the middle of the night on Mother's Day. I gave the eulogy at his funeral and wrote it in the middle of the night with a flashlight in the middle of a basketball court at a local park. I had so much anger and hate towards him and it took me some 25 years to finally let him go. I'm pretty sure he has watched out over me during all of my terrible accidents as I could have been killed in any of them. I held my abusive father's hand 10 years ago as he took his last breath and have never shed a tear for him. This past Spring in my meditation space I finally let him go also. I realized how much of my power I had been giving away to him and my traumas. My mother quit drinking about 20 years ago and today is one of my best friends and the best grandma ever to my children.

I was in the car business for 9 ½ years from age 20-30. It was the only business I know of that would allow me to drink the way I did and would turn a blind eye as long as I kept the cars rolling off the lot. I had the look and gift of gab and became successful moving through the ranks to General Sales Manager of a large Honda dealership in Memphis, Tn. My then wife and I moved there chasing her career in television. She eventually took a position with a TV show in California and we moved to Burbank when I was 29. My drinking really took off there and that is when I had my moment of clarity/my bottom. I remember looking in the mirror after another night of drinking and realizing I had finally become the man I told myself I would never become…my father. I was a drunk, liar, master manipulator, and thief. I had focused so much energy on what I didn't want to become I actually manifested it to be.

I started going to AA meetings and knew I had found people who were suffering just as I had been. I worked the 12 steps with my sponsor and went to some 600 plus meetings that first year. It gave me a foundation that serves me to this day as I am about to celebrate 20 years of sobriety on November 18, 2019. However, my struggles with life and relationships was difficult and I continue to struggle at times. I divorced the first wife, remarried to the mother of my two

Amazing children for 14 years (many separations during that time), joined a religion I did not believe in for 8 years, remarried again after that to someone with issues I could not accept, and now I am on a spiritual journey to find happiness within myself as I have decided to no longer look externally for Love or Happiness. Learning to forgive myself and to Love myself has been the most rewarding relationship I've ever known. Once I had my experience with Oneness and my heart was blown open I realized I had been living a lie by not believing in myself and walking in my Soul's Purpose….My Truth!

So, what happened that turned my life around? Where is the hope I can offer for those of us who had childhoods/lives like this? How in the world can a person like me be successful? So, during all of this craziness my false ego was in full swing and helped me to find the energy and will to push myself in business. I quit the car business for good in 2000 and I started my career in real estate as a realtor. I had finally found a home as I quickly realized I didn't have to sell anything but Me. That I could do as my false ego could win people over. I had just moved to Sacramento after marrying the mother of my children and I knew No One. When I started diving into my new career, I had a fairly successful first year selling 17 homes but my second year I sold 55 houses with zero online presence. During that second year I was asked to manage a small office which I did. I attribute this quick success to hard work as I did things no one else wanted to do. I foot walked 250 homes a week with door hangers and would do it around 5pm so I could catch the owners coming home from work. I realized I did not need the name of the big company as my business did not skip a beat. The market in Sacramento was taking off and I could feel it. I took the money I was making and invested in my first property. I flipped that property 14 months later and netted over $100k. I was hooked and never looked back. Just after year 2 I got my broker license and opened my own office bringing a team of agents with me. I also open a mortgage company with the help of someone who is now my best friend. By 2008 I had flipped some 30 houses, had 35 agents under my license, had a successful mortgage company, a family with two step sons and my own two children, callings in my church, coaching my children's sports teams, and volunteering in all of my kid's elementary classes. I can't remember ever missing an assembly where one of the kids was getting an award.

I knew a very successful commercial developer and constantly bugged him to invest money in house flipping and he eventually gave it a try. We ended up flipping some 150 houses over the next 7 years or so on nothing but a hand shake. I had a lot of his money out on properties in my name and all on trust. Nothing is worth losing the trust of people you do business with. Being successful is All about how you treat people and building relationships. I've now lost count at over 340 homes I have flipped in the greater Sacramento area and feel so blessed to do what I love for a living. I have people who trust me with their hard-earned money to make extra income by flipping houses with me. I love making other people money and giving back. I've made a great life financially being fearless and taking risk. If you can't believe in yourself then Who Will! People all around me want to do what I do but very few will take the risk necessary to set themselves free financially. I set my own hours, have passive income, attend all of my kids events, coach their sports when asked, give myself a raise when I need one by applying more effort, and I have started traveling around the world this year as I explore the deeper parts of my soul and the true purpose for being here……to help others Evolve to a Higher State of Consciousness! To help humanity to let go of the domestication we have been brainwashed with and to step into themselves in their Truest and Highest Potential.

I now believe each trauma, abuse, neglect, and abandonment we experience in our early years steals a part of our souls as we are just not capable in human form to handle that much pain and fear. I feel if this did not happen, we would die or go crazy as many do. I have two beautiful souls who have tag teamed me in my spiritual recovery….Kadea and Nicolle. These two spirits know me better than anyone on earth and I cannot give them enough credit. I Love Them Both Dearly. I want to say that I am not writing this chapter for any other reason than to advance the expansion of Love, Compassion and Kindness I have for all beings, creatures, animals, plants, oceans, rivers, trees, water, air, and insects within this Eco System we call Earth. To help people Wake Up and Remember Who They Are is a calling I feel deep within my heart and soul. I believe we were all born with the Divine inside us. The Inca's call it 'The Inca Seed' and it is called many other names around the world. I feel our purpose here is to not just make money, have a career, buy a house we never really own, raise kids, and die. That just sounds terrible and sad to me. But to know myself on a soul level and walk in my Truth is to taste the nectar from the Divine Mother's finger tips. I need to heed Her call these days like I need food and water.

I've been called many things by friends and those who know me best and I guess the one that resonates with me most is "Warrior". I don't give up easy and I will fight for Truth. I don't have anything I'm trying to sell you here, no website to direct you to, no workshops to attend, and no anything other than praying my message gives one person hope to go deep inside and believe in themselves and let go of life's experiences that have held you back from being Authentically You! To Walk Upright Before All in Your Divine Truth and Glory is My Humble Prayer. Do that and you will be rich beyond anything you can accumulate in this existence. And Maybe, just Maybe you will be blessed to do what you love for a living as a result. Abundance is there for us All! We need only 'Let Go' of the past and follow our heart's call. So, stop denying that still small voice inside you and give it the stage it deserves as it calls to you. My earth name is Marty Scott Daniel but if you be so brave to step out of your comfort zone you can address me as "Ocean Eagle". A spirit name given me by a beautiful soul named Linda Star Wolf while attending The Gathering of the Shamans in Sedona, Az. I resonate with autonomy in my spiritual journey as I am looking into all modalities to find my Truth in this regard. I will be in Peru to learn from the Q'ero Indians this month, Teotihuacan in Mexico to learn the Mayan ways and Shamanic Breathwork in Nov-Dec this year and Egypt in 2020 to go home to my ancient family there and remember the Mysteries there. Being a successful entrepreneur has given me a life beyond my wildest dreams. May you journey to find Your Truth and Your Financial Freedom let you Dream!

With all the Love, Light and Blessings I can send you I say Namaste!

***

To contact Marty:

Email: oceaneagle018@gmail.com

Facebook at Marty-Ocean Eagle Daniel

.

Robert Proctor

Robert Proctor is the CEO and President of MultiSoft Corporation, an international MLM Software provider to the industry since 1987. Since 1999 Robert has been involved in the launch of over one thousand Multilevel Marketing Companies. Robert has been a keynote speaker at the MLM Startup Conference in Las Vegas since 2012.

He and his company have been involved in nearly every aspect of helping clients launch their network marketing companies. From consulting to software and e-commerce to directing website and UI design, setting up server farms, compensation plan review and design, sourcing logistics, how to hire the right staffing, print media, developing onboarding systems, and much more.

Robert attributes his success and the success of MultiSoft to his mentor and retire founder of MultiSoft, Peter Spary, who left him with a simple principal of "Did you do what you said you would do".

Married to his wife Susan for 21 years, his personal motto of *"you have to give what you've got, to get what you give"*, a principal he taught early on to his son and daughter, have allowed him to practice servant leadership on behalf of his clients, his church, and the Boy Scouts of America.

Should I Start a Network Marketing Company?

By Robert Proctor

*"If you want to be successful, you have to Jump,
you have to take a leap of Faith"*

— Steve Harvey.

Hello, I am Robert Proctor, and I would like to start by saying if you are considering starting a Multilevel marketing company, congratulations!

My "formal" education certainly did not prepare me for the network marketing industry or the knowledge and relationships I have developed over the years, which are necessary in the industry today.

"Formal education will make you a living; self-education will make you a fortune."

— Jim Rohn.

No truer words were ever spoken to describe the industry of Multilevel Marketing. Unfortunately, you won't likely find any formal classes in high school or college that will teach you how to launch a network marketing company. So, you must work with people that have "the right stuff," and can take you from vision to success, and from concept to commissions.

When consulting, I tell clients "I have been involved in the Network Marketing Industry since I was four years old". This is my earliest memory of mom and dad dragging me to Tupperware home parties with them. However, my path to becoming an industry leader in network marketing was not overnight and was a rocky one at best. In fact, in my early 20's, during my time in corporate America, while working for one of the nation's largest banking institutions, I become so disenfranchised with Multilevel Marketing, I thought I had sworn it off forever.

I have had the opportunity to work with the best consultants, attorneys, and 3rd party providers in the multilevel marketing industry. Since 2012 I have also been fortunate to be a keynote speaker at the MLM Startup Conference in Las Vegas, where I also maintain a staffed office.

Should you choose network marketing you will be entering an industry where your sole responsibility will be to empower and inspire others to see your vision. Done right, it can be the most personal and financially rewarding experience of your life. Done wrong, it can be costly in time, money, and reputation. Network marketing is about education, communication, duplication, and compensation.

If you have a product or service that provides value to others and you desire to financially impact the lives of thousands, potentially tens of thousands, of individuals and their families, by helping to put a few hundred or even a few thousand extra dollars in their bank account each month, then continue reading.

If, however, you are looking for a way to make a quick buck or generate enough money to buy a new Rolex or a fancy sports car, I recommend you stop reading and become a sales representative or distributor, and NOT start a network marketing company.

I'm sure that we have many common traits. First and foremost, you are an entrepreneur at heart. You envision a better life for yourself, your family, your friends, and for others. You want to impact the lives of others positively. That you are teachable and willing to take risks, to achieve your dreams and life goals.

Truth be told, my "unofficial title" is "Psychologically Unemployable Serial Entrepreneur." Every day I get to work with entrepreneurs just like you, I experience enormous satisfaction helping to put individuals in business, helping to keep them in businesses, and, most importantly, helping them to grow their businesses.

In many ways, we're being forced into entrepreneurialism, because the dream of a rewarding future, upward mobility, and an exciting career is fading more and more every day. Large traditional businesses can no longer guarantee salaries or security. The payoffs today are layoffs, stagnating careers, and organizational politics.

So much for a secure career these days. The sooner you face the fact that employers can no longer fulfill your expectations of personal success and financial security, the sooner you can move forward with the decision to doing something about your future.

So, what is the answer? Owning a multilevel marketing business is a viable way to control your own destiny. The goals of meaningful work, personal satisfaction, and control over your own life can be achieved if you own your own multilevel marketing company, and it's easier to get started than you might think.

So, precisely what's involved in starting your own multilevel marketing company?

You will need a degree of entrepreneurial spirit, a mindset that gives you the confidence to work with people, and the motivation to pursue your dreams.

It will be much easier if you can rely on a proven support team to help you grow your business.

Vision and Management

Management is the brain of your company. Without it, the company will blindly stumble around without purpose, conviction, or direction. While disagreement among management can be healthy, the management team must share a Common Vision.

The first thing you should do with your new company is to establish the "Management

Vision"; what the company is, and where it is going. Once the Management Vision is set-in-stone, you are ready to bring in management personnel to help drive the company towards its intended Vision.

Key behavioral qualities

Preparedness, on your part, to be coached by industry professionals is essential to your

success.

Persistence and focus on work habits are essential because MLM is not a "get-rich-quick scheme."

MLM is a legitimate and legal business marketing model. Government regulators require MLM providers to prioritize retail sales and focus less on recruitment. Pyramid schemes are now outlawed in most, if not all, countries.

MLM relies on building networks of people who sell products to the end-user, through a network of independent contractors, referred to as Distributors. It is an established multi-billion-dollar marketing strategy spanning the entire world, and many experts predict that MLM could outpace franchising as a business model.

MLM organizations recruit individuals to act as independent distributors. These distributors are paid commissions on their sales and on the sales of those in their organization. At its heart, distributors operate as self-managed entities.

A motivated entrepreneur can easily set up a network marketing company

MLM, as a business opportunity, has a low start-up cost and relies on the ability of individuals to recruit distributors and actively build relationships that foster win-win scenarios for all parties.

It reminds me that entrepreneurs are the doers of the world. And, it makes me think of what someone once said about people in general. "Folks are divided into three groups. Some spend their lives doing things, others have things done to them, and the rest watch."

The great Dr. Norman Vincent Peale says, "I want to tell you about the two most powerful words in the world. The first has only five letters, but it has the strength to move mountains. That word is called "FAITH." Faith in yourself, faith in others, faith in your abilities, and faith in your future. If you don't have faith, who will have faith in you?" For you, the entrepreneur, that faith must become second nature.

Then he speaks of the second of the two most powerful words in the world. So powerful, that if you allow it to, it can wipe out faith. That word is a four-letter word called FEAR, fear that you can't be or do something, fear of the past and its consequences, fear of tomorrow for what tomorrow might bring, fear that you might fail.

Joe Girard, an exceptional salesperson, says you should:

1. Believe in yourself.

2. Associate with confident people.

3. Tune up your confidence machine.

4. Be master of your ship.

5. Keep busy.

MLM is for you if you can master these simple 5 Key Requirements.

Helping you control and conquer that self-destructive fear is the purpose of this chapter "tune up your confidence machine" and be the "master of your ship" by turning fear into faith and confidence, with the knowledge you WILL turn your Vision into reality.

Software solutions must be combined with a comprehensive business solution and a support service plan, because of the extraordinary failure rate of start-up companies.

According to the U.S. Small Business Association, 90% of start-up ventures fail during their first year of operation. The common reason for the failure is that a significant percentage of people cannot fathom or manage all the nuances and requirements inherent in a new business venture.

First, let me make this very clear — starting a multilevel marketing company is not easy, and the only way to make it easier is to surround yourself with brighter, more intelligent, and more experienced individuals, that have "been there, and done that."

Starting a network marketing company takes hard work, and it takes smart work. It takes perseverance and determination. Your family and friends will probably think you have lost your mind. For the first year, you can expect 7-day work weeks and 18-hour work days. It requires real relationships with vendors, distributors, customers, and employees.

It takes customer service skills. It takes empowering others and stepping out of their way so they can lead. It takes a complete absence of greed and ego. It takes relying on other's ideas and suggestions and knowing which ones to listen to and which ones to disregard. It takes pushing down arrogance and stupidity.

It takes recognizing that distributors, the ones leading the charge and following your vision, are independent sales agents. Your distributors are your "volunteer army," not your employees; and in today's gig economy, they have alternative choices.

Yes, it takes money, which is your least concern. Money is easy, everything that comes along with it and what you do with it is what matters.

Every MLM company's mission should be to sell products and services.

With all the hype and hoopla that surrounds MLM, it really boils down to one thing and one thing only: Sell your products and services before all else!

Towards that end, MLM companies are no different than their counterparts who have chosen alternative methods by which to market and sell their wares.

Think about it. Is Walmart, a giant in retail sales, in business to make clever commercials, and promote smiley faces? No, of course not! Those things are merely support tools for their real

purpose of selling product and generating corporate profits.

As a current or prospective MLM company owner, you cannot let yourself become mesmerized by the hyperbole of the industry. You must stay focused on the end goal of making sales.

The easiest way to maintain focus is to think strictly in terms of survival. Question: What is the one thing that you cannot remove and still have your company remain intact? Answer: Its products and services. MLM companies are sales organizations. Without a product to sell, there can be no sales organization and therefore, no company.

Choosing a viable product or service, understanding it, and making it salable is the foundation for your success. Focus on the merits of your product or service before getting caught up in lifestyle and double back-flip bonuses, and your chances of building a successful MLM company increase exponentially.

If you are contemplating the launch of an MLM venture because you are under the "get rich quick" ether, stop now and save yourself time, money and heartache.

The cornerstone of any successful MLM company is its product and service offerings. Whether it is a single dynamite product or an entire product line, a viable product is a surefire way to make repeat sales.

Pressure selling may well cause people to join your company initially, but only great products or services will motivate them to continue selling.

Bottom line: substance sells.

As the CEO and President of the leading global software provider to the Multilevel Marketing Industry, MultiSoft Corporation (in business since 1987), I can tell you that massive action is the only action that matters and the one single step you should take to succeed.

> *"There are no shortcuts.... There are 4 types of action; retreating, doing nothing, normal action, massive action"*
>
> *— Grant Cardone.*

Since 1999 I have been involved in the launch of over one thousand Multilevel Marketing Companies. I have been fortunate to be involved in almost every aspect of helping clients launch their network marketing companies. From software and e-commerce to directing website and UI design, setting up server farms, compensation plan review and design, sourcing logistics, how to hire the right staffing, print media, developing onboarding systems, and much more.

Today, unfortunately, less than ten percent of those one thousand companies are still in business. Why did some succeed and many more fail?

I have witnessed companies with arguably the best compensation plans and most unique products and services, close their doors within a year. I have also worked with companies that have the craziest compensation plans, and products, you could find anywhere and not know anything about Multilevel marketing. Incredibly they became highly successful.

What was the difference between the ones that succeeded and the ones that failed?

Simple, it was leadership and momentum! Their achievements came from working with and listening to the right industry experts. They recognized they *"did not know what they did not know."*

As an example, I worked with a company several years ago that had grown to over fifty-thousand distributors and over sixty-million in sales, in under a year, and then just six months later closed the doors. How could a company get this large and then fail? Simple, they changed the distributor compensation plan even after they were advised not to.

Success came to those individuals that understood the "value" they must provide in an industry which flips the typical corporate America businesses model upside down, by embracing the fact that they are in the network marketing industry. Yes, product sales are of primary importance, but network marketing is all about relationships. Be passionate about your relationships!

"Train people well enough so they can leave, treat them well enough, so they don't want to"

— Sir Richard Branson

I don't consider myself to be the "typical" consultant, who wants to keep themselves "on the drip" for as long as possible by pointing out problems that you are then responsible for solving. Instead, I think of myself more as a "connector," as well as a coach, trainer, or mentor.

My responsibility to my clients is to share my experience, knowledge, successes, and failures, and connect you with the right people and the right companies that will work to help make you successful.

Most "consultants" tend to look at things with the mindset of "If it is not broken, don't fix it." Whereas I look at things with the mindset of "If it's not broken, did we try to break it? If it's not broken, when is it going to break? And, if it's not broken, when is it going to be outdated or replaced?

Benjamin Franklin said, *"By failing to prepare, you are preparing to fail," and later Winston Churchill modified that to "Failing to plan is planning to fail."*

However, this infers, that if you plan to succeed, you won't fail. If you want your plan to be successful, plan it, monitor it, and manage it, or find people that will do it for you.

My Eagle Scout son taught me the 5 P's: "Proper Planning Prevents Poor Performance," which sums it up better than Benjamin Franklin or Winston Churchill ever did.

If you are going to fail, and you will from time to time, you need to learn to "fail often, fail fast, and learn from your failures." I believe Nelson Mandela said it best with "I never lose. I either win, or I learn". When we stop learning, we start dying, and you should spend time everyday learning.

Consider the following few questions to gauge whether you are failing to plan or planning to fail and whether you have considered the 5 P's I mentioned earlier:

—   What is the difference between Direct Sales, Multilevel Marketing, Affiliate Marketing, and Influencer Marketing?

—   How much mark-up from your COG (cost of goods) to the retail sales price is needed to generate commissions and yet remain competitive and profitable?

—   Do you know how to design and implement a compensation plan that will reward, recognize, and incentivize your distributors?

— What is the difference between a "legal" MLM and an "illegal" MLM (a pyramid or ponzi scheme)?

— Do you believe your corporate attorney, who set up your corporation, knows anything about compensation plans, product claims, or the states you must register as an MLM?

— Is the bank where you have your personal and business accounts at going to provide you with a merchant account for your Multilevel marketing company?

— How are you going to find, and more importantly retain, customers and distributors in the ever-growing gig economy?

— Do you need a National Sales Director? Where are you going to find him or her?

— What do you "need" versus what do you "want" from a software provider and how important is it that the software is scalable and intractable with other platforms?

— How are you going to pay commissions to your distributors?

"Did you do what you said you would do?" — Peter Spary

These were the words the founder of my company, and my personal mentor left me with since retiring in 2010.

These are the words I think of every day when I wake up and when I go to sleep every night; "Did I do what I said I would do?" Did I return all of my calls, did I answer all of my emails, did I deliver to my client's expectations, did I do the best I could?

Whether you are just "dipping your toe in the water" to find out more about an industry that has over 150 million people worldwide, 18.2 million (in the USA alone), generates over 200 billion in worldwide sales, with more than 34 billion transactions in the USA in 2018 alone, or whether you are ready to "Go all in" I know you can use some help and guidance; connect with me via my contact information below.

"Say Yes, Tell the World, Figure It Out"

— Eric Worre.

***

Robert Proctor – CEO and President – MultiSoft Corporation

http://www.mymlm.com

http://www.mlmstartupguide.com

http://www.multisoft.com

http://www.marketpowerpro.com

http://www.mlmbuilder.com

robert@multisoft.com

O: +1 239-945-6433

M: +1 239-839-4904

Jeffrey K. Mack

Jeff Mack is a devoted husband, father, and thirty-year entrepreneur. After receiving a Bachelor's Degree in Civil Engineering, and spending a few years in the Real Estate Development and Construction industry, he became intrigued by the world of direct sales. In his twenty plus years as a top field leader, Mack achieved Top 10 Earner status in three different companies. He was named "Most Valuable Leader" in one of those. Mack has served as an advisory board member for several large companies and has built international sales teams of over 25,000 people, resulting in total sales in excess of $250,000,000. Mack founded his own direct sales company and served as CEO for over two years. With his unique experience as both a successful field leader and running a start-up from the corporate side, Mack formed Global Growth Consultants in 2014 to utilize these talents and his knack for successful international expansion. Global Growth Consultants was established to help companies control costs, increase efficiency, and improve their overall performance while increasing revenue and growing their global footprint, simultaneously improving the experience for the reps in the field. Mack is a sought after speaker and trainer, known for his humility, down-to-earth style, professionalism, and ability to connect with his audience.

Failure is Part of the Process

By Jeffrey K. Mack

To Crack the Rich Code, to me, means to become an entrepreneur; start a business, whether you have a job or not. If you have a job, great! Perhaps you're unfulfilled in some way. Maybe you're not making enough money, have too much stress, no time, freedom, autonomy, a hostile work environment…could be anything. One thing's for sure. You're reading this book for a reason. I'm not suggesting you put your family at financial risk by quitting your job prematurely; in fact, quite the opposite. Be strategic about your future, how you're going to create it, and when you will venture out on your own as your main source of income. Bottom line, a little sincere planning, backed up with focus and perseverance, will go a long way in reaching the goals you have for yourself, your family, and your future.

Now before I go further, let me address the definition of the word "rich." Usually that word is associated with making a lot of money, and that's cool if that's your goal. However, to others, living a "rich" life may mean lots of travel, time spent enjoying their kids and family, and creating memories on their own schedule. There's plenty of people that would LOVE that. Maybe to you it's both, or something completely different. Whatever it is, get clear on what you want, then you can make it your future reality. You'll have to be in charge, because "rich" means you call the shots in life, and in order to do that, you'll have to *be* the boss, not *have* a boss.

I'm sure you've probably heard all this before. You may also have already tried your hand at having your own business. Perhaps you've hit a wall and can't break through. Or you've failed and are second-guessing whether you have what it takes. Whatever category you're in, know this: you're not alone. I want you to know that you already have everything it takes to succeed, and consequently, to also fail miserably. That sounds daunting, but also empowering!

You merely have to guard, protect, and fully utilize those assets and your odds of success will skyrocket!

What I'm referring to is your mind—your thoughts, and most importantly, your imagination. Let me explain. I began my adult entrepreneurial quest at age twenty-five. Yes, I sold Christmas cards as a child, had lemonade stands, and would even go hunt lost golf balls and sell them back to the golfers on the same course. But as an adult, after stumbling my way through a Civil Engineering degree and working in that career for a few years, I was impatient. The logical thing for me to do was to pay my dues, learn the ropes, then start my own building business and eventually become a developer. I have friends that took that route and have done incredibly well for themselves. Me, I was impatient and perhaps lacked vision. Whatever it was, what I was doing at the time didn't "speak" to me. I needed more action, the ability to set my own schedule, and work from anywhere. It sounded incredibly glamorous!

After being given a video tape of a direct sales (multi-level marketing) company, I bought-in to the concept and saw the possibilities. In fact, after attending a large opportunity meeting, I really bought-in—and when I say I bought in, I mean I swallowed the hook, the weight, the whole damn fishing pole. As per my advice above, I started building my business at night, after coming home from my job. I got so revved up, I started to build that business while I was at my job; not exactly the best way to impress the boss. Bottom line, I quit (or got fired…who's keeping score?), and after a few months, I was building my network full-time. Within a month or two more, I was earning enough in my business to support myself; I was single at the time. One of the benefits of being single was not having a lot of responsibilities, so I could live a spartan existence, which was key to early success in my opinion.

Yep, I was self-employed. Sounded great. Glamorous, it was not. I actually moved back in to my parents' home and set up their basement as a little office; my own personal boiler-room. I would make sometimes up to 250 cold-calls a day. It wasn't easy. The single word to sum up this period, the start-up period, is *sacrifice*. When I say sacrifice, I mean long hours and missing fun social events. It was all-encompassing—total immersion. Thankfully today, technology and social media make the "blunt-force" approach look silly. However, regardless of how and what you decide to build, sacrifice is one of the earmarks of any entrepreneur's success.

Back to the imagination. Once I began to see a little success, after the first fifty-four people I called about my business told me no, I finally heard the word, "Yes!" When that happened, it was like someone threw a bloody fish into a shark tank. I was focused and locked-in on the scent. I won't bore you with more of that story, but I do want to give you a synopsis of my first ten years. After switching companies, in my second full year full-time, I earned over six figures in my direct sales business. That was a lot of money in 1993! Then, it multiplied as I diversified my business geographically and got the "international bug." In 1997 I earned 7-figures; I felt ten-feet tall and bulletproof. I had arrived...or so I thought.

By the time we built and moved into my dream-home on Lake Norman, my income had begun to go backwards a bit, and the armor had a bit of a chink in it. What I didn't realize was that it was all going away...all of it—the home, the Harley, the business, my marriage, all of it, and it was MY fault. The direct sales company I was a distributor for, got purchased, merged, and sold. The name changed, and the compensation plan changed multiple times. It was an amazing case study on what *not* to do as a company. However, even with all of that, my circumstances and how they affected me was MY fault, and looking back on it, it is crystal clear today.

Rather than cut my lifestyle back, take the cash-flow and money I made and start another business that I could build in conjunction, I found myself searching for another company one after the other, where I could instantly get back to the level of income I needed. I had been betrayed by professional colleagues I called friends, some of which I had known for decades. Rather than take this as a sign that I needed a different environment and needed to use my imagination to reinvent, I tried to use the one trick (skillset) I knew and apply it by doing the same thing in a different place. In looking back, that would have actually been enough; except, I wasn't willing to swallow my ego, cut my lifestyle back, and dig in. I was entitled, a bit scared, and turning my back on the cornerstone of my original success; the development of my mind and imagination. Rather than look at the role I played in my downhill slide, and what could I learn from it, I passed it off as everyone else's fault. I stopped reading positive messages and books—stopped feeding my mind with things that built me. Instead, I started doing things that made me feel good in the moment, but left me empty inside.

Finally, after a few years of going through the motions, I was presented with the opportunity to start my own company in the industry where I once had so much early success. The idea was amazing and the products we were selling were on point. By every right, we could have, and should have, been a smashing success. However, my mind wasn't right, and I still had yet to face the reality of what needed to be done. I made quick decisions, rather than sustainable ones, and went against what my gut was telling me. Actually, looking back, I am proud of what we accomplished. It just wasn't enough. Thus, for a number of reasons I won't get into here, this venture was the most public and loudest failure of my career. It was a gut-shot that still leaves a mark. The humiliation almost got the best of me. I fell into a deep depression, and for a while, kind of rolled around in my own self-pity. I guess you could say that the onion got peeled back enough to finally force me to ask some tough questions. After having a marriage failure a few years earlier, the financial hit that goes with that, and a few business and investment failures, something amazing happened.

I guess you could sum up the turning point in my life with one word: love. I began to really notice and appreciate the love that was shown to me by my family during this time of uncertainty—especially when I actually didn't really love myself. When I wasn't looking for any romance and didn't think it would ever be something I'd be interested in again, I found someone that I had fallen in love with. After thinking I would never be a father, I found out I was going to be the dad. When my daughter was born, I found a love that I could never begin to describe. All of this strengthened my soul, my core, and I literally was given a new lease on life—kind of a do-over. While, what I describe as, the downward spiral was over a 10-year period, the ascent was less than half the time. This time, it came with a new, welcomed friend: gratitude. I found myself grateful for all the blessings I had in my life, rather than focused on what I didn't have. Granted, it's a daily struggle, but the difference gratitude and happiness make in our lives can't be overstated. It does, however, need to be experienced to be really understood.

Throughout these four years, I became reacquainted with the power of my thoughts and how they affect my life. I found myself reading again and was reminded of how little decisions every day compound and lead us over time to the results that we experience each day— not from yesterday, but from months and years earlier. With love came gratitude, then action, then confidence, and finally, back to imagination. All of these are too often taken for granted. I know first-hand. But when you lose them, you recognize the difference; often times, after the fact. Either way, if you find this story a bit familiar, have hope. Sunshine is on the horizon and maybe it's only an honest look inward away.

Since then, life, business, health, and happiness are all on the upswing, and I can honestly say that I am a better person, husband, father, and professional for having experienced these trials. Since this book is called, "Cracking the Rich Code," I'll mention that YES, each of my last few years have been better and better financially. I've got some exciting projects in the works, including a more detailed book on the mental journey I went through, along with those of other successful entrepreneurs. I want it to be a roadmap—no, a treasure map—of what to do and what to avoid while creating your entrepreneurial journey.

In the meantime, here are a few of my biggest takeaways and most important tips:

If you're not growing, you're dying. You can say this a thousand different ways. The bottom line is, nothing stays the same—not people, not plants, not the universe. Change is going to happen. If you're complacent, the dynamic will work against you. Take your body for example. If you do no physical exercise at all for months on end, you will change, and not for the better. You may gain weight, you may or may not look any different. But inside, your bones, joints and muscles will atrophy. Keep that up for years and see how you look a decade or two later. Conversely, let's say you train or at least get some light physical activity in regularly. Your bones and connective tissue, along with your muscles and joints will be better off, and your heart will most likely be healthier. A decade later, and your active self will be in much better condition, health-wise and appearance wise; it will make a big difference in how you see the rest of your life and even how long that may be.

Now, imagine what a difference that can make in your brain, since your actions and nearly everything about you starts in your brain. You don't want to let that atrophy. Just as physical activity is good for your body, positive stimulus is good for your brain. Try this. Just read something positive or productive for fifteen minutes a day. You can even read some fiction, as that too will stimulate your imagination. Just stay away from negative subjects and publications like newspapers or gossip magazines. Read about a subject you have an interest in, and after a few weeks, before you know it, you'll have finished the book and learned some new things. I'll bet you'll feel better too! Feed your mind good things to grow in the direction you want; which brings me to my next subject:

Associate up, not down. Just as putting the right input into your brain and body will make an impact on your output, spending time with the right people will also pull you in the direction you want. It's often said that your net worth will likely match the average of the people you spend the most time with. It's true. If you want to accomplish things, hang out with ambitious people. If you want to live a fulfilling life, hang out with those that want the same. Whatever you do, limit the time you spend with negative people. So first, figure out what you want, which is a key to success unto itself. Then, put yourself in that environment as much as you possibly can. Do this, and you'll likely see magic happen over time.

Build a network of allies that lift you up. Similar to the above, people that enhance who you are on a personal level are the ones you should keep in your life. However, there are those who can also enhance you professionally. They may or may not be the same people. For example, if you are a real estate agent, get to know a good real estate attorney and other individuals that make up your professional network: such as contractors, plumbers, electricians, handy mean, etc. These will be people that you rely on to help you and your clients. Build good relationships with them. If you have a personal relationship, great. Regardless, make sure they are dependable, competent, and that they know how much you appreciate them. When you need them in a pinch, having this network in place will prove to be an invaluable asset.

Live frugally and save, save, save! As a successful entrepreneur, when things are going really well, you become tempted to think that the money will just keep coming in forever. However, for most, it doesn't. There are seasons of feasts and seasons of famine. I made this mistake and have seen countless others doing the same over the years. You never know when you're going to hit that season of "drought." Maybe it's a market crash like in 2001 or 2008. Maybe it's a government regulation that impacts your business. Maybe it's your company being sold, and the ensuing upheaval cause your income and cash flow to suffer. How will you handle it? Personally, I have lived through all of the above scenarios and more. When the income slows down or stops, the bills keep coming. If you have cash in the bank, that's great. If you have cash in the bank and you are still living below your means, then you can begin to become bullet-proof. Two resources I suggest: *The Richest Man in Babylon* by George Clason and *Unshakable* by Tony Robbins. Do yourself a favor. Invest 4 hours and read both of these books. Apply what you learn, and you'll be prepared for what comes.

Sometimes, you have to give it to God. He knows what you need. Whatever you believe in—God, the Universe, whatever—it's worth believing, it's worth having faith in. There have been times in my life that I absolutely had no idea what was going to happen or how a situation would work out. Some of those things worked out great. Others seemed to work out horribly for me at the time, but with hindsight, I can see that it turned out to be the best outcome in the long run. What I learned from that is, all we can do is all we can do, and you have to have faith that hard work, integrity, and continuing to strive will be enough. It will. Have faith!!

***

To Contact Jeff:
Jeff@JMack.com
JMack.com
http://linkedin.com/in/jeffreykmack
Twitter: @JMackGlobal
https://www.facebook.com/JMackGlobal/

David Volpe

David Volpe spent 30 years in the Financial Services industry. During this time, he was a private wealth manager for individuals and business owners. David also acted as a Financial Consultant to public and private companies. In this role, he assisted companies by connecting them with different sources for raising capital through relationships he has developed over his long career. David always had a passion for Technology and recently decided to leave the Financial Services industry to pursue his true passion of being involved with a Technology company in a totally different role than his previous business. Currently David is involved in a Venture with his new business partner, Joel Sauceda that is soon to be announced! David Lives in Arizona with his wife of 20 years, Amanda Volpe and his three kids, Kristin, Austin and John.

Goodbye $ Hello @

By David Volpe

The Entrepreneurial spirit has been alive and well in my family since its inception many years ago. My Grandfather immigrated to the United States from Sicily in 1927, he was 14 years old. He worked as a Barber during the day and went to school to learn English at night. He lived in Queens then found a job in the garment industry. He eventually went into business for himself.

My Father was a retail pioneer. His concept was years before discounters like TJ Maxx and Ross came on the scene. We had 7 stores in the Valley of the Sun in Phoenix and lived a very good life during those years with ZERO competition. This family business paid for my brother and I to go to private schools and eventually college. The retail business can be extremely rewarding financially if you have an original idea but when the competition comes and has deeper pockets than you, it can kill your business and eventually kill YOU! My Father did all he could to compete but as more and more of these giant retailers started opening everywhere the stress finally got the best of him and he died of a massive heart attack at 49 years old. Almost done with college I knew I wasn't taking our over stores and staying in retail. The retail chapter was over, and my chapter and my business life were about to begin.

It was the summer before my last year of College. While I was home visiting, I spent some time with an Uncle of mine, and he asked what my plans were after I graduated. I was just thinking I would have a degree so I would get a job no problem. He invited me to spend some time over the summer at his firm. He was a Financial Advisor. So, I spent almost a month there and I absolutely loved it. Especially the idea of trading stocks. At the end of my time at his firm, all his co-workers encouraged me to get licensed and come work with them. When he said I didn't need my degree to work there and I could start making money right after passing my tests I was intrigued. Then I decided I wasn't going back for my last year!

I attended classes to prep for the exams. I learned about traditional Financial Planning Methods, Managing Money for clients and how to manage risk in a client's portfolio. I was told to plan on failing the exams the first time around because they were so difficult! I was never good with tests, but I passed them all the first time. Trading stocks is what excited me the most but everything I had just learned after passing my exams wouldn't have helped anyone, let alone me! There were no books, classes or exams that could have prepared me for what I was about to embark on. There were no history books or professionals that had ever seen a period like the 1990's before.

The first 10 years of my 30-year career went by like a weekend! The Dot Com Era began in 1990 and ended March 18th of the year 2000.

My Uncle's business exploded about the same time I started. If he was on a call, our receptionist had instructions to send the call to me. After a while those clients started calling me directly and he just told me to take them over as clients. Back then at most big firms, a new guy or gal would just make cold calls all day long to build their practice. I was also given a handful of accounts to start working with and built it into a large list of clients very quickly. The rest of my clients came from referrals because of my trading ability.

Not all advisers trade stocks. Most buy and hold stocks if they're decent companies or they put together a portfolio of diversified Mutual Funds and then move on to finding the next new client. It also takes serious balls to trade stocks because if you don't make people money you lose your clients.

Two types of clients make up your practice when you manage money. Younger, still working and willing to take risk and those that have made all their money and just want to protect their investments and live off the income. My practice was about 80% retired clients and 20% younger risk takers that wanted me to trade for them. The ability to grow people's money is an incredibly powerful talent. Managing the 80% retired was easy for me. The other 20% were totally different clients and they expected a lot from me! I delivered and got a lot of new clients because of it.

The 20% occupy 10 years of my life!

I was one of two young men working at a firm with all 50+ year old individuals who did traditional financial planning. I was obsessed with technology companies. I was already following companies like Microsoft, Apple and Intel but those weren't Dot Coms. I teamed up with the only other young guy at the firm and we set out to find the hottest stocks of the future. We worked in cubicles right next to each other and we passed ideas back and forth when the first company we didn't know announced they were going public. Who the hell is Amazon and what do they do? Online retail something I say!

We would throw names around and acronyms became our new language. All the hot new tech companies traded on the NASDAQ and most had four letter stock symbols. This stock index was all electronic unlike what you see on TV with all the people walking around on the floor of the New York Stock Exchange. It was fast so when you hit the BUY button you better be sure you entered the order right because in about 2-3 seconds you now own whatever you entered! Here's an example of what can happen: Symbol for Intel is INTC. Stock Symbol for a Telecom company back then was INTL. If you buy the wrong stock and have to "Break" the trade and there's a loss, you eat it. If there is a gain, "The House" keeps it. Never thought that was fair but ok!

 AZMN, hit that up! What's that, he would say, and I'd say check the balance sheet. He was a great number cruncher and I was communicating with multiple Hedge Fund managers I had contacts with throwing symbols back and forth. Then my partner comes back with "this company is total Shit, Next! Business model won't work, and they are going to lose money for the next 3 years. I call out AOL to him. What do they do? I say ISP and he says "WTF is an ISP!" (internet service provider, what you use to connect your device to the internet) He comes back with "Yo Dave, for real? Same shit business model, this stuff is garbage, no proven history and you wanna buy these things?" Yes, it's what people are calling about! Most of the veterans at our firm scoffed at the idea of investing in non-profitable companies. My young counterpart and I knew that we had to take a chance. What if it wasn't a fad and what if this was the future of investing that could last a long time?

We split the entire tech sector in half. We had a list of companies that already went public and were trading and a calendar of what companies were coming public. Every day we each brought our half in and what we decided to trade. If I didn't know a company, he did and if he didn't know a company, I did.

I developed a network of traders, hedge fund managers and venture capitalists. We all communicated via AOL Instant Messenger before the open, during the trading hours and for many hours after the market closed. Sharing ideas and resources gave you an edge and we weren't competing with each other, so it was worth it for all of us to share what we were trading and why. This network eventually developed into a website called The Street.Com. It was founded by former Hedge Fund Manager Jim Cramer. This site became the first and last stop of every day because real traders and money managers were writing and posting blogs in real-time all day long there.

Anatomy of a Trade-Dot Com Zone!

The typical day started at 5:30 am being at the office waiting for the market to open at 6:30 AM Arizona time. At the bell we place trades. A typical IPO (Initial Public Offering) would hit the market anywhere from $50-$100 a share. It went something like this: A stock opens and starts trading at $80. We buy. Two hours later sell at $120. Buy back at $130. Ninety minutes later sell at $160. One hour later buy it back at $190 and then before the close blow it all out (sell) at around $230. That's an example of trading one stock during market hours. We were doing this same trade with 5-6 different stocks all in the same day and in multiple client accounts!

There were days when we did this, and a stock would open at $60 and close the day at $300 a share. This was the new normal. The other advisors that watched this happen and said it couldn't last were eventually right, but they missed 10 years of making big money for clients and now I had a reputation for profitable trading. My practice kept getting bigger as people got more and more overcome with greed. At this point any advisor not willing to trade Tech was losing all their younger clients to advisors like me. At any given time, I could rattle off 20 ticker symbols I planned to trade in the next 24 hours!

This went on for almost 10 years and then the day came that paying for research actually paid me back and saved my clients millions in losses. By this time, Jim Cramer's TheStreet.com now had a paid section of the site. This was now the only place for real-time trading insights from some of the smartest in the biz and I was happy to pay for access. In February of 2000 Jim Cramer called "The Top" of the market and said it was time to get out. None of my clients argued when I said its time to sell everything. He had been right so many times I wasn't going to second guess his call; everyone out and into cash.

Enter slow motion Dot Com Crash!!

After about 30 days and finally getting to breathe again in cash after 10 years of this non-stop trading, it finally came to an end. Traders and investors got tired year after year of being told by companies the business models would work and they would eventually all be printing money. Now the Dot Coms were out of time and shareholders were out of patience. March 18th of the year 2000 marked the beginning of a selloff that lasted two years. The market went down every day for two years. It was like walking into work and being sucker punched out of nowhere every morning. All you could do was watch. I was thankful I avoided losses and the clients I gained during this period were now mine for life!

Now What?

We went from a period of Tech only investing to people not wanting to hear Dot Com or Technology ever again. As a money manager your job is to find the next new trend. I always followed Commodities but never had enough of a reason to want to jump in. Enron ring a bell? This was a company that analysts were afraid not have a buy recommendation on for fear of being called out by the company Enron itself.

So, Enron collapses and now every energy company, power producer and oil refiner are corrupt? Not so fast! Do we not need power anymore? No need for oil, natural gas, gasoline? In this business you can either complain that you got the trade wrong, or you can see the opportunity in the midst of a crisis or company scandal and capitalize on it. I always choose the latter. After the collapse of Enron, it was just an Enron problem, yet every refiner and power producer's stocks were reduced to single digit stock prices. You can't just paint an entire industry with the same brush when one company's balance sheet was a total lie!

Enter the Energy and Hurricane Trade!!

The collapse of Enron affected every stock in the same industry. How many other Enron's were lurking? None! Time to put on another big trade. The collateral damage was so big in the wake of Enron that there were stocks that were trading in to $50-$70 range that were reduced to $5 and $6 a share in a matter of days while the dust settled. We put together a list of about 10 stocks in the single digits and bought them all. Only one of the 10 filed for bankruptcy and the it wasn't because of anything Enron related. About 9 months later nine of the ten we bought had going back up to more rational pricing and we made a killing.

At the same time this trade went into play I watched energy prices climb in 02, 03 and in 2004. I decided to enter the Crude Oil market along with Natural Gas, Refiner stocks and Unleaded Gasoline. It seemed to me that during Hurricane Season from June 1st to November 30th any time there was a hurricane and the Gulf Coast had to shut down, it would create shortages in these commodities and prices would go up. Why not load up on Natural Gas, Crude Oil and Unleaded Gasoline? They seemed to be the most affected by shut down fears because of hurricanes. Answer? Buy and Hold Crude Oil, Natural Gas and Unleaded Gasoline every year starting June 1st and not selling until November 30th. Putting on this trade in 02, 03 and 04 made some decent gains so we kept putting it on every year. When you have conviction that a big trade is possible you keep trying it until it works, or you decide it was a good idea but it's time to look for another trend. I knew this trade wasn't over, but I didn't know the magnitude of how big it would be. It turned out to be the last trade in the sector for me! Why tempt fate!

In 2005 Hurricane Katrina hit New Orleans. It was a historic year for profits. Our younger clients were heavily invested in Crude Oil, Natural Gas and Unleaded Gasoline. Overnight Natural Gas went from $3-$15 a BCU (Billion Cubic Feet). 2005 was a hugely profitable year.

I was paid to make people money. That was my job. I didn't think about whether or not I was investing in Tobacco, alcohol or other socially irresponsible sectors. No one cares where their capital appreciation comes from as long as they are making money. I don't care what people say in public because everyone has a level of greed that appeals to them.

Yes, I'm that sure. So, make the biggest bet ever!

After the Dot Com Bust, I had the confidence to invest or trade anything you could trade. I did my homework and my due diligence and recommended the best opportunities I could find for my clients. Next up? My last big event I'll ever deal with during my career, The Financial Crisis of 2008. In the fall of 2007, I started seeing cracks in the financial markets, hedge funds going under and not being covered on the financial news and in the Real Estate market. I moved my trading clients all to cash not knowing what was going to happen, but it looked like something bad was brewing.

I was both fascinated and obsessed with the events that occurred in 2008. How could things have gotten so out of hand? How could these Financial Firms and banks get themselves into a situation like this? Well, they did, and they almost took the entire world Financial system down with them.

This was a period of time that saw dramatic declines in bank and financial service company stock prices. Companies like Goldman Sachs, Merrill Lynch all the way to Bank of America and Wells Fargo and JP Morgan Chase. All these companies' stocks went down into the single digits except for JP Morgan Chase that bottomed around $13. The question was: Will they be bailed out? If the Government decides to make a statement and teach these companies a lesson for over leveraging and taking on too much risk these companies could be wiped out along with their companies' stocks. If they get bailed out, then their stocks will spike back up so fast that you won't be able to buy in fast enough. The risk? I have to buy now in the single digits and wait to see what the Government does.

There was no way to gain an edge, either do it or don't but you have to be in before it's announced. Then we got the first hint, Bear Stearns. This over 100-year-old company was gone overnight. Then Lehman Brothers which in my opinion was an experiment to see how it would affect the financial markets and it didn't go well. I also think it exposed a preview of what was to come if a company this size went under. Everyone else after Lehman was huge. No way can they let a bigger company go under just based on the collateral damage Lehman caused. I'm all in! I called a small group of my younger clients and told them my plan. We're not just going to buy stocks this time, we're going to use leverage and buy Call Options on top of buying their company stocks. I picked 4 stocks. Bank of America, Wells Fargo, JP Morgan Chase and US Bancorp. I bought all of them in the single digits except for JP Morgan Chase, I bought that just under $14. I never had this much client money concentrated in so few stocks. The problem with options is that they have an expiration date. If you buy a 30-day option and it doesn't do what you hope it does in 30 days they expire and your money vanishes. If the option trade works, you control large amounts of stock without having to put up as much money. So, options combined with stock is either going to make you a hero or a goat!

29 Days later, no sleep and 10 pounds lighter, the Government announces a bailout for the banks and the financial service companies. To illustrate the power of leverage, my best friend inherited $440,000 from his Grandmother in the summer of 2007. He wasn't going to need the funds for many years and wanted me to trade for him. In 2008 I invested his cash. From when the bailout was announced, a little over year later his $440,000 was worth $1,600,000.00.

These are just a few highlights over a long 30-year period. It wasn't all about trading, although it was at times. I wouldn't recommend this business to any one I know now. I developed a lot of deep friendships with multiple generations of families. I watched investments I made for clients when their kids were born pay for their college, weddings, houses and vacations that were planned for years. I enjoyed working for myself and the ups and downs that came with it.

There was also a succession plan in place with my Uncle. I would inherit his practice when he retired, and this came into play a few months ago. Having a successful practice of my own was great but to inherit his practice on top of my own would be a dream to any Financial Advisor. Unfortunately, I had to decline taking over his practice. When you are passionate about a business you should do it. When you lose that passion like I did about 2 years ago, you need to find something else you are passionate about and I have done just that! I wrote earlier about how much I loved Technology, and I still do!

There's an amazing guy I've known since the 90's. He has a Technology Company out of San Antonio. We've done some ventures over the years and we always talked about doing more together but I never had the time. Now I do because he ignited that passion again for me and he has asked me to be the CEO of his company! I'd like to say thank you to my Uncle, James Rapisarda for helping me write the first Chapter of my Business life, mentoring me and also being a great friend! And I'd like to thank my friend and NEW Business partner, Joel Sauceda who will help me write the next Chapter of my Business life! Change is always a little uncomfortable but it's good for you! One constant that never changes no matter what is going on is the patience and understanding I've gotten from my wife of 20 years, Amanda Volpe, You're MY Rock, Thank you, and I love you!

***

To Contact David:

David@DavidVolpe.Com
dvolpe@cox.net
DavidVolpe.Com
602.380.4824

Elaine "Lainey" Lien

Lainey Lien is a multi-certified career services professional and personal brand strategist with a strong commitment to and broad range of experience in coaching, training, and speaking. She is the founder and CEO of ReVive Careers and co-author of the book *Translate Your Personal Brand into Marketing Magic©* coming summer 2019.

After many years as a successful corporate professional in a wide range of industries, Lainey caught the solopreneur bug in the early 2000's and has never looked back. Today, she combines her real-life experiences with her vast career management training to help senior level managers and executives fine-tune their careers, enhance leadership performance, develop their personal brands for professional success, find and land new jobs faster, and create work-life harmony.

With her mantra "committed to your success," Lainey believes in providing a personal and upbeat approach tailored to meet each client's needs and goals. She thoroughly enjoys working with open-minded, enthusiastic, and action-oriented professionals. Her clients have said, "Working with Lainey is like having a coach, therapist, and friend rooting for you all at the same time."

Lainey specializes in career management, leadership development, personal branding, job search strategies, DISC assessment training, and professional speaking engagements.

Put Your BRAND to Work for YOU

By Elaine "Lainey" Lien

Early on in my entrepreneurial journey as a newly certified coach –
I think the ink on my certificate may have still been wet, absolutely
excited to apply all the training I had over the past year, and
chomping-at-the-bit eager to get my business going – I dove in head
first! I decided to attend a small women's conference in my area.
The room would be filled with women of all ages in different stages
of their careers. *This* would be my golden opportunity to meet oodles
of professionals struggling at work, ready for a new job or to make
a career change. I came prepared with a stack of business cards to
hand out to the dozens of women who would line up, anxious to
meet me and beg to become one of my clients right then and there.
I felt like a kid in a candy store; I could barely contain my
enthusiasm!

I settled into my seat in the front row and chatted with some of the
women around me. The presenter appeared and provided us with
information about the day's events and expectations. And then, IT
happened. She said, "To get the most out of your experience and
help you feel more relaxed, we encourage you all to get to know one
another throughout the day. We've known some women who have
gone on to be long-time friends. Some have even started businesses
together." That sounded right up my alley! Not so fast. She followed
up with, "To help you get started, let's go around the room and
introduce ourselves. We'll start with *you* here on the end. Would
you be so kind to start us off?" Wait! What? Me? Noooo! She *was*
pointing at me! You know that heavy, paralyzing sensation you get
in your legs when you suddenly wake up from a nightmare? I felt
every bit of that.

She said, "Please stand up and briefly tell us about yourself and what
you do." This was THE holy-cow mother of all questions! "Tell me
about yourself" has been known to drop a grown man to his knees
and stop the best of us in our tracks like a deer in headlights!

Not only did she want me to go first, but she wanted me to stand up to tell – to what seemed like thousands of "successful" women – about myself! I was not prepared for *this!* I was only prepared to hand out business cards at break time to the flock of women begging to work with me.

I had two choices at this point; I could either run out of the room waving my hands in the air screaming "F I R E," or I could stand up and blurt something out. How hard can that be?

I blurted something out all right – something to the effect of "My name is Elaine Lien I prefer you call me Lainey all my friends and family do I am a new career and leadership coach and a longtime resident of Denver I live with my hubby and two amazing kids…"

And, it kept flowing out like blood from the deepest papercut…

"…I love gardening and interior design I wanted to be an interior designer when I was younger but that didn't happen because of where I lived none of the colleges in my state offered it and at the request of and out of respect for my parents I stayed local to complete my 2 years of basics first but actually ended up pursuing a degree in healthcare instead oh and I really enjoy running which is actually more like a jog-run which I call junning since I have asthma."

Notice no punctuation marks anywhere in that "Run, Forest, Run"-on sentence. OH, YES, I actually said this!

Now, I could have been wrong, but I thought the conference hall had an infestation of crickets, because I heard an orchestra of them as I stood staring at the presenter's expressionless face. After a long pause, she said with a question mark in her voice, "Thank you…Diane." Diane? Really? It's Lainey. For the rest of the day I was known as Diane to those few women who spoke to me out of pity, I was sure.

Needless to say, there were not any fans lined up to take my card or sign up for my services. My debut moment to shine, to fill my coaching practice in one swoop, make my mark, and stand out, to tell my would-be tribe who I was, what I was very good at, and how

I understood and could solve their problems was GONE! It had been completely extinguished with my broken-fire-hydrant-sized ramblings. I should have yelled "FIRE!"

As I sat there in my humiliation, I listened as some women gave nerve-driven responses, while others delivered a one-and-done. That is how you do it – powerful pitch with clarity and confidence. This was a wake-up-slap-in-the-face moment for me. I came with the assumption once people knew what *I* did, I would be a rock star. I was a career and leadership coach after all. Did that not sell itself? The smack-upside-the-head reality was I clearly did not know what was so special about what I had to offer. What did I have to offer? What made me different or stand out from the next career and leadership coach? Um…? There were those darn crickets again! Wasn't this room full of my ideal clients who needed me? Who were my ideal clients anyway? The pitch-perfect women delivered clear, confident, and compelling speeches in 20-30 seconds. How were they able to do that? They seemed so matter-of-fact and certain. *I want clarity! I want to show my confidence! I want to be compelling!* But, how do I do that? How do any of us do that?

Read On…

Let me be clear, this chapter is not about crafting your elevator pitch (I'll save that for a chapter in my next book, *Translate Your Personal Brand into Marketing Magic©* coming summer 2019). There is a ton of moving parts and a lot of work to be done before you can eloquently blurt out your super-entrepreneur-hero declaration (wish I had known this before I went to that conference!). However, what I will be focusing on is the importance of *discovering*, *defining*, and *delivering* your **personal brand** – *the foundation of your "tell me about yourself" story.*

Let's get personal!

What is Personal Branding?

What comes to mind when you hear the word "branding"? Do you think of celebrities, athletes, or big companies? Do you think of it as being only for those with deep pockets? That is how it used to be.

The concept of personal branding has been around for the better part of the last century. However, the popularization of personal branding came into the spotlight in 1997 with the article written by American businessman Tom Peters for Fast Company magazine called "The Brand Called YOU." Since this explosive article, personal branding has become a household name for most entrepreneurs, solopreneurs, freelancers, and now professionals – job seekers, career changers, and leaders on the move, anyone who is looking for the secret formula to stand out from the competition and be seen.

As someone who is in business for yourself, what kind of feeling do you experience when you are told you need to build or create a strong personal brand in order to grow your business? Does it feel like an exhausting, daunting, or painful process? Do you feel like it is a load of you-know-what, and you will get along just fine without it? Do you equate it to having to go to the gym, immersing yourself in intense exercise programs to build your branding muscles?

Let me reassure you, while your strengths are a big part of your brand, there will not be any weights or strenuous exercise involved, unless you just really like that kind of thing. And, there will not be anything to build or create. So, you can put your hammer and glue gun away. Personal brands are not built or created. They are *realized*, *developed*, and *evolve* over time. Your very personal brand already exists inside you whether you know it or not. YOU already have everything you need.

Personal branding is the process used to help you "discover, define, and deliver" your personal brand to those who need to know you. This is where you determine how you differ from your competitors and learn to take the necessary steps to stand out in this noisy world. The branding process puts you in the driver's seat, allowing you to take control of your direction. If you are not an active participant in your branding, others will do it for you, which may do more harm than good to your reputation. Take control of your brand's reputation now in order to reach your ultimate destination – success.

Personal brand is your unique combination of your skills, talents, passions, values, personality, quirks, strengths, and weaknesses, too. Together they make up your unique promise of value which is delivered to and experienced by others through your actions, reactions, and interactions.

Your unique personal brand is the magic ingredient that

helps differentiate you from the competition.

As entrepreneurs your personal brand is ***the heart and soul of your business***. Your personal brand gives your business life. It is the blood, sweat, and tears that run through your business's veins, the heartbeat of your business. Sounds quite important, doesn't it? Here is the thing; most people will associate a business with the person who started it all. Its founder is the face, feel, and "differentiation factor." Oftentimes it is the person who sits at the top of the company, the CEO, and this may be the one who brings the business to life.

It has never been more important for entrepreneurs or solopreneurs to develop and take charge of their brands. A recent study commissioned by Upwork and Freelancers Union revealed freelancer's entering the market in growing numbers. Projections indicate that within the next decade, freelancers will make up the majority of the workforce. This means competition for similar products or services will become much more saturated and intense.

Here are a few benefits to developing and taking control of your brand:

- Attract more of the *right* clients from your ideal target audience.
- Boost your level of recognition.
- Command higher compensation.
- Manage your reputation.
- Build confidence, credibility, and trust.
- Form mutually beneficial partnerships and alliances.
- Open the door to more speaking opportunities.
- Set and accomplish more career-directed goals.

Starting to get the picture? If you are not absolutely clear on *who* you are, the significance of your personal brand, or you are struggling with forward momentum in your business, listed below are 3 basic steps to help you start unpacking your brand. These steps begin the process of fleshing out the answers and putting the pieces together to effectively deliver your clear, confident, and compelling brand for greater visibility, recognition, and success.

Let's unpack Personal Branding 101. Here we go…

Step 1: Discover – Who are you?

Hint* You are not your job title.

The **Discover** step is where you will spend most of your time in the beginning. This crucial step is often skipped or ignored by those eager to get going and start doing. Do not skip this step.

Before taking off on a journey, flight attendants tell us, "In case of an emergency, oxygen masks will drop. Place the oxygen mask on yourself first before assisting other passengers." Translation: you must take the time to understand and care for YOU first before you can fully understand and care for your clients.

❖ Take a look at *why* you do what you do. What motivates you? How do your values play a part in everyday and long-term decisions? Think about your greatest accomplishments - determine what super-strengths you used to make them happen, and what weaknesses showed up. Identify the types of people you enjoy being around and the environment you thrive in. What is the most important thing you want people to know about you? Get to know your personality and quirks. Why do you need to know about your quirks? Here is an example:

> As my husband playfully pointed out, I eat in circles. I generally start with my least favorite item and work my way around the plate to my favorite. I apparently do the same with hamburgers – start on the outside, work around until only the yummy center is remaining. What does this have to do with my brand? This little quirk

translates across to the way I go about most things. When tackling any project, I typically start with my least favorite tasks first – get 'em out of the way. I prefer to save the best for last. This gives me a sense of accomplishment and something to look forward to. I finish my day off on a positive note!

Get to know yourself and what makes you tick. You may be pleasantly surprised by what you discover.

Oscar Wilde said it best, **"Be yourself, everyone else is already taken"**

Step 2: Define – *What is your Differentiation Factor?*

This is where we come back to the surface. Hang on, we are not quite ready to go full frontal with your brand just yet. In the first step you spent time mining your inner most self for answers. Now let's get into more of the nitty-gritty stuff.

The **Discover** step is about "Who *you* are." In the **Define** step it is about, "Who *they* are, why *they* should care about you, and how you differ from the competition."

- ❖ **"They"** = *your i*deal target audience - the people whose problems you are in the business of solving. Why should **they** care how you solve their problems differently than others? Clearly define who **they** are and what problems or challenges keep them up at night. What makes you qualified to help them? What are you currently known for? What do you ultimately want to be known for? Who are your competitors (this will require a bit of sleuthing on your part)? What do you do or offer that is different?

Do your due diligence; get to know everything about who **they** are and why **they** need *YOU.*

Step 3: Deliver - *All right, Mr. DeMille, I'm ready for my close-up.*

Now you can go full frontal - with your brand, that is. In the **Discover** step you started to get some clarity about who you are and what makes you tick. In the **Define** step your uniqueness started to shine through; you began to build your confidence by understanding who your target audience is and how you differ from your competition.

- ❖ The **Deliver** step is about bringing it all together so that you can deliver a consistent and compelling message to the world, attract the positive attention of your ideal clients, and repel those who are not. In today's highly visible world, it is much easier to be found, which can be good (or bad) depending on how you position yourself on- and offline. To be compelling, *authenticity* is key! Let your personality shine through. Share information and ideas and become active in your market. Form alliances and join groups with other like-minded folks.
- ❖ You gotta spend money to make money…yeah, yeah…no, seriously - Invest in YOU! Hire a graphic artist to help you visually deliver how you wish to be perceived through your brand style: colors, logos, website, marketing materials, and signage.
- ❖ Do not go looking for clients in all the wrong places – All the style in the world will not do you any good if you do not have anywhere to show off your new outfit! You must learn where your clients are hanging out (online and off), and where the best places are to spend your marketing bucks. For example:
  - ➢ The majority of my executive clients use LinkedIn for professional networking and job searches.
  - ➢ If your ideal clients are moms, you may find most of your audience on Facebook, Pinterest, Instagram, Snapchat, and probably not on LinkedIn.

In order to be remembered as clear, confident, and compelling, all verbal and visual messaging needs to be consistent. Make them remember you as the one who solves their problems and genuinely wants to help them improve their lives – the expert in your market.

Let's wrap it up

I find time and time again, those who have dedicated time to developing their brands, are those who have a clear path to moving in their desired direction and accomplishing their goals. If you are struggling to attract the *right* clients, not making the kind of traction or impact you desire, or feeling a bit of a disconnect with your business, I strongly encourage you to take a closer look at your personal brand. If after going through the steps presented here you find you need additional help, don't worry. This process is challenging, but you don't have to do it by yourself. Consider hiring a personal brand strategist or coach to guide you through the process of Discovering your *who* and *why*, Defining your "differentiation factor", and *how* to Deliver your authentic message consistently to your target audience. Coaches can be a true asset to helping you develop your marketing strategy and plan, reach your goals, stand out in your market, and reconnect you with your business, ultimately, shedding new light on *you* as the bright shining star you are!

You never know when your golden opportunity will present itself, when it does – make sure you're prepared…with more than assumptions and a stack of business cards!

Now, go put your brand to work for YOU!

***

To contact Elaine "Lainey"

www.revivecareers.com

elaine@revivecareers.com

LaineyLien611@gmail.com

303-668-6760

www.linkedin.com/in/elainelien/

Lisa McDonald

EMPOWERING business owners, individuals, and entrepreneurs to transform their lives, achieve their goals and turn their dreams into realities by walking the talk and approaching life, love, and work with FEARLESS gratitude, enthusiasm, and hope.

Through her suite of services including coaching, mentoring, and her top-rated podcast and online TV show, Lisa McDonald inspires people to do and be their best every single day.

Lisa's approach is simple, and yet profoundly impactful. She will empower and re-invigorate her audience to take daily action in their personal and professional lives.

She proves that by moving away from fear, anxiety, and overwhelm, even the newest online entrepreneurs can generate exciting momentum as they move closer to building a life and business they love.

Living Fearlessly with Lisa McDonald

By Lisa McDonald

Entrepreneur is not a word I take lightly nor is Entrepreneurship a journey I take for granted. It is an all-encompassing, all-in, full-throttle five-star recipe of blood, sweat, tears, and continual sacrifice, and most definitely not an arena to be played in or embarked upon for the faint-hearted. The quitters and the impatient get turfed/weeded out; swiftly.

Entrepreneurship at the core level, is not a buzz word, a trend, or the flavour of the month. It is the Olympic Games every single day and not something you have four years to train for the day of. The day of is every single day. You are training, performing, and aspiring to break world records in a succession of 24 hour intervals. To even compete at this level, one must specialize and excel in a plethora of required areas while operating and executing with a multitude of skill-sets.

As a serial solopreneur, (and there are many of us) the level of self-discipline has to be fiercely insane. There's no one hovering over you, micro-managing you, telling you or reminding you of what you have to do, how to do it or when to do it - there is no official performance appraisal for checks and balances - there is no excuse-making, or sick-day-taking. YOU ARE IT - 24/7! So when did I decide to embark upon the maniacal world of Entrepreneurship? Would it surprise you to know that I did so during the same time frame of my Mum dying, my Grandmother dying, my husband and I heading down the aisle of divorce, and embarking upon single parenthood with my children then aged 3 and 18 months old - yeah, seemed liked the perfect time! And in all honesty, it truly was.

Having previously worked as a Director/Senior Manager specifically in crisis management, within the world of social services, in addition to my own backstory/life experiences, which taught me at the early age of 4 years old (that's another story which you can find on Amazon #LivingFearlessly) what it inherently meant to rely upon myself, to believe in myself, and to un-apologetically lay claim to my place in this world. No surprise and no coincidence that my personal brand is Living Fearlessly with Lisa McDonald. More than a brand, more than my global radio show/podcast, TV Show, my books, my speaking engagements, my roster of mentoring and coaching clients - Living Fearlessly with Lisa McDonald encapsulates my DNA, my mindset, my verbiage, my approach and my outlook on daily life!

As someone who consistently interviews top-tier, notably named thought leaders, world renowned celebrities, and extremely successful entrepreneurs, (including both the phenomenal Jim Britt and Kevin Harrington) I am not one to be enamored by names and titles for names and titles sake - no, what impresses me at the core of who people truly are - are those who are genuinely #LivingFearlessly. Those like myself who thrive off of risk-taking, momentous growth, rapid expansion, rigorous hustle, insane grind and who are results driven and outcomes oriented. These are my Tribe and Vibe Attracts Tribe and if that were not the truth, my name, and my chapter would not be a part of this awesome book! Jim, Kevin and myself would not be playing in the same sandbox, let alone travelling at Mach speed on the trajectory of success!

In a world of Gurus and Experts professing the importance of being in the here and now, I will admit to you, that I am not. I am forever living in the future and this mindset has served me well, hence having both the capacity and the capability to effectively serve others equally well. When one truly grasps how fleeting and invaluable each moment of each day we are afforded the additional gift it is to be here - there is zero time available in which to waste or to take for granted. As someone who has perpetual lofty goals, as someone who is always looking to outperform and upstage myself - I never make the counter-intuitive or foolish presumption that I can postpone, cancel, delay or squander today in place of there being a supposed tomorrow. None of us knows when our time is up, and so knowing this to be an absolute truth, I non-negotiably kick it into high-gear - ALWAYS!

Once upon a time, I used to say that there were never enough hours in the day. This declaration then advanced to my saying that there were never enough days in the week. These constant time constraints were impeding my output so what does an Entrepreneur then do...an Entrepreneur who is committed to being solution focused as opposed to problem saturated? They invent an eighth day for themselves by waking up at 4:00 each morning. You multiply an extra few hours a day X 7 days a week (because Entrepreneurs do in fact work 7 days a week, and on holidays, and on birthdays, etc...) - there my friends, is your solution to increasing your output and sooner receiving your achievable results and outcomes. And who thanks you? Your FUTURE self thanks you!

As someone who is consciously mindful of Legacy and what it means for me personally, I inherently understand and embrace that my Legacy is wrapped up in who I choose to be, who I can anchor, who I can empower each and every day. Those days add up over a lifetime and so when one decides to LIVE and to LEAD 24/7 X 365 days per year - that is massive value and immeasurable impact one has committed themselves to for the purpose of paying it forward and being of service to the collective. Does this equate or translate to 'Making A Difference' in this world? The obvious answer is of course, YES! How could that level of persistent contribution not make a profound difference to the overall well-being and benefit of others?

This brings me to PURPOSE! Anything (including and especially so in the business world) that derives from or is birthed out of PURPOSE has teeth - has legs - has vision - has sustainability - has longevity - has momentum - has direction - has focus. Purpose underscores everything which is substantiatively meaningful. Again, another buzz word often times thrown around like a football by most who have zero intentions of advancing to the Super Bowl - harsh as that may sound - it is the truth. Once I became exceptionally clear on what and who future Lisa looked like - my Purpose organically and authentically emerged. My inherent purpose is to 'Uplift You To Fear Less And To Live More!'

I put my transferable skills under the microscope, conducted a serious evaluation on myself as a genuine leader and agent of change, assessed the timeline of where I had already embarked upon this mission albeit differently illustrated as a Senior Manager working within crisis management with those who fell within the 'isms' of our society. I expanded the base and the reach so I could effectively impart my mission of #LivingFearlessly with the masses. It was during this reinvention process; a re-birth if you will; that I was incredibly attuned and tapped into my own pain - two back to back deaths, the death of my marriage, catapulted into single parenthood...the crisis spotlight had now shone brightly upon me. Who takes care of the caregiver dichotomy, right?! And so it began...

The life lesson I have most paid attention to throughout the course of my life and have incorporated into my honed business mindset is this - When one chooses to tap into their pain and bridge it with their identified purpose - boom, bang, you become UNSTOPPABLE!! Not only do you become masterful at solving your own pain - you become sought out to facilitate, navigate, and maneuver other people's pain. Who cannot relate to pain? Who has not experienced or endured pain either at the emotional, physical, spiritual, financial, professional, personal, relational level? No one is exempt or immune from being in the abyss at one point or another in life. For me, and my brand of #LivingFearlessly knowing that my purpose with and for the collective is to 'Uplift You To Fear Less And To Live More' - that means everyone on the face of this planet is a prospective business partner, global radio/podcast guest, a mentoring/coaching client and the list continues. Is that cold? Contrived? Disingenuous? NO - it's truth and I always honour my truth! To you the reader - what is your truth? What is your purpose?

Bottom Line - If I am an expert at anything...it is being the Master of Turning Shit Into Gold! And truly Mastering Turning Shit Into Gold has been my ticket to 'Cracking The Rich Code!'

In my life-long worldly experience on Planet Earth thus far, I have calculated that there are three distinct pods of people. There are those who are addicted to their pain and who are more invested in staying there (I do not associate with these people either personally or professionally). There are those who acknowledge their pain and who are genuinely invested in flipping that pain on its head and turning it into purpose (my Tribe). Lastly, there are those who learnt this invaluable lesson long before myself, and who have become my Mentors (my Alignment Family). This is my formula for discerning very quickly who stays - who goes - and who I hustle to get on the radar of! This formula works if you choose to employ it!

And because my Super Power is Turning Shit Into Gold - the naysayers, the critics, the jealous, the insecure, the resentful, the negative have indirectly become my biggest fans and staunch supporters for propelling me further and farther on the trajectory of my success. When they go low - I go higher! It truly has become a win win scenario for me and so I thank everyone equally and genuinely for their contributions. The sky isn't the limit - BEYOND the sky is the limit hence LIMITLESS!

So...let me provide you with a tangible example of how I have made this all work for me. People love stories and I like to tell them, write them, and live them. And I also like to share the wealth...after-all, we don't know what we don't know.

Four years ago when I was initially sought out by the first radio network who wanted to partner with me (am now partnered with two global radio networks, which is phenomenal marketing and promotion for all my weekly showcased guests) this was never looked upon as a hobby for me. This was the beginning of what has now gone completely vertical for me as a viable business model - intentionally, deliberately, and strategically so. I sought out at the very early stages; knowing this would take me 'awhile' to accomplish what I wished to futuristically cultivate and garner for myself, to relentlessly go after those in the space who had once upon a time been an intangible mentor for me. These were notable, world renowned people whose books I had read, YouTube videos I had watched ad nauseam, masterminds I had attended - you name it - I was immersed in the world of personal growth and personal development so as to eradicate and excise my own 'cancer' aka pain. I wanted to maximize all my platforms so as to individually express my wholehearted gratitude to these pivotal mentors of mine and to enlighten them as to the very specific ways in which they had profoundly shifted my emotional state within all aspects of my life.

I started with Dr. Deepak Chopra. It took me a couple of years to land him but I did. Then I went after Leeza Gibbons who because of my credibility and success of securing Dr. Chopra - was an immediate and resounding yes to appearing as my guest on radio. To date, my roster of featured Living Fearlessly with Lisa McDonald global radio/podcast guests includes: Jim Britt, Kevin Harrington, Les Brown, Les Brown Jr., Jay Shetty, Jack Canfield, Daymond John (pitched him in person in NYC at a C-Suite Network Thought Summit), Dr. Wayne Dyer's daughter, Serena Dyer, Zig Ziglar's son, Tom Ziglar, Jeffrey Hayzlett, Kyle Cease, Dave Pelzer ('A Child Called It') Lolly Daskal, Don Miguel Ruiz Jr., Dr. David Suzuki, Keith Perrins Jr., (Daymond John's FUBU counterpart), a handful of Tedx Speakers (one who used to work security detail for Tony Robbins and who was also the last person to deplane from the aircraft that became known as #MiracleOnTheHudson - now my C-Suite brother), Marci Shimoff, Ben Gay III, Dr. Marshall Goldsmith, and the STELLAR list continues.

Oprah, as everyone who closely follows me would know, knows, that she is my number one intangible mentor and the ultimate guest I aspire to interview on Living Fearlessly with Lisa McDonald. Have I landed her as of yet? - no - however, I do speak with two of her direct personal assistant's on a quarterly basis who graciously and who legitimately pass along my correspondence, my gifted books, and my regular updates to her directly.

Fast forward to approximately two years ago. The lovely, and iconic Arianna Huffington, who personally (not her team) generously offered me the gift of being a fellow contributor to her phenomenal global site, Thrive Global, as a blogger. Fast forward to only a handful of months ago - Arianna amazingly circled back with me and further gifted me with the opportunity to showcase my Living Fearlessly with Lisa McDonald radio/podcast guests on Thrive Global inclusive of my personally written Feature Article, citing my takeaways following each guest interview, inclusive of the corresponding podcast link, along with the professional show graphics with embedded photos of my guests head shot in addition to whatever it is they are specifically recognized for or wishing to showcase - their book, a product, them speaking on the stage, and so forth. As if that was not already beyond over-the-top generous of Arianna - she had also lifted the Thrive Global protocol of my content having to go through an initial 'Pending Publication' Process as per the usual procedural standard prior to content upload and visibility on the Thrive Global site. Arianna waived that prerequisite for me. When someone like Arianna Huffington gives you the keys to her car - you know you have established trust, legitimacy, and credibility. JUST WOW!

I want to be perfectly clear here. Every single guest I have ever interviewed on Living Fearlessly with Lisa McDonald has brought something profoundly significant to myself, the loyal listeners and the podcast subscribers - regardless of whether they held international, household, notable name recognition or not. Irrelevant. However, what is relevant and what has strategically worked for me hence ALL my showcased guests are my having amassed a generous following, and standing out in an over-saturated industry of well over 600K Global Podcasters. A space which is growing exponentially every single day. And as a result of having one world renowned leader after another showcased on my show specifically (not an easy feat by any means) - my name being attached to their name has infused massive growth in my numbers, my daily stats/metrics for how my show ranks in 145 countries via Apple (rankings have varied between #83 to #350) out of almost a million podcasts flooding the market.

Living Fearlessly with Lisa McDonald has now become a 95% referral based business. The tables have turned. On a daily basis, I have Publishers, Publishing Companies, PR people, inundating my inbox with requests for their clients, authors, speakers, bloggers, coaches, celebrities, and CEO'S to be considered as a prospective guest on my global platforms. On average I am booking two to four guests each week, and am oversubscribed (booked up months in advance) for each guest's appearance. To keep up with the volume and the influx of those wishing to be showcased, I have had to open up a second air-wave slot on the networks; bearing in mind of course, that this is only one hat I wear as a serial solopreneur in conjunction to being a single parent which is and always will be - my number one priority. Today's results and today's reality was my projected future, and only four years ago when I initially embarked upon this journey. Truthfully, this is me, only scratching the surface for where I continue to project and envision the future of Living Fearlessly with Lisa McDonald.

Howard Stern has talked candidly on his own podcast about the near impossibility of podcasters monetizing from podcasting. I believe he may have even cited that those who do and can are within the minute 1% of the podcasting community. I am beyond grateful, honoured, and humbled to say that I am one of those podcasters who is in that 1%. I am a pay-to-play business model. In my personal life, I have always been charitable in nature. Fundraising, donating, contributing, volunteerism has and will always remain a big part of who I am at the core of who I am. However, business is business and my business is not a non-profit. I would never expect or ask a fellow entrepreneur to carry me, pay my way, or give me a free pass on their own dime or at their own timely expense for my own gain or advantage. That is not the spirit of entrepreneurship. Occasional bartering of services? Sure. Flexibility of an offered payment plan? Sure. Freebie? NO!

When previously showcased guests are willing to pay a second or even a third time to appear on your platforms, that is an endorsement and a half as to the value, impact, results, and opportunities they received and benefited from, let alone anything else to appropriately substantiate the rate of return on the rate of investment. Results don't lie and only those who are truly #LivingFearlessly trust and believe in themselves to the degree of taking one risk right after another. Entrepreneurs are unique in the fact that we wholeheartedly subscribe to the old adage and key principle, which is, 'You have to believe it to see it!'

My secret sauce for which I am consistently sought out for is my recognizable and innate ability to make others shine, stand out, and stand apart even from others who are perceivably doing and saying the same things. I know how to put the spotlight on others in such a rare, no holds barred, #LivingFearlessly approach that my clients and guests fall back in love with the essence of who it is they really are, which becomes their superpower for scaling and leveraging all aspects of their life. It doesn't get more yummier than that!

If there is anything I can do beyond what I have already shared, imparted, and offered within this chapter to further propel YOU on the trajectory of your own life and futuristic vision you have downloaded for yourselves, it would be my pleasure to connect with you and shake things up!

Be Your Own Hero. Be Your Own Shero. Be Your Own Leader. Be Your Own Best Friend!

Uplifting You To Fear Less And To Live More!

Love & Gratitude ~

***

To contact Lisa:

Http://livingfearlesslywithlisa.com

https://lisamcdonald.ceo/

Weekly Email Tribe: Fear is a Choice Email Tribe

Facebook: Living Fearlessly with Lisa McDonald

Twitter: @FearlessLisaM

Instagram: @FearlessLisaM

LinkedIn: Lisa McDonald / LivingFearlesslyWithLisa

You Tube: Living Fearlessly with Lisa McDonald

Google + Living Fearlessly with Lisa McDonald

Thrive Global: @FearlessLisaM

Medium: @FearlessLisaM

C-Suite Radio: Living Fearlessly with Lisa McDonald

About the Show:

"Living Fearlessly" with Lisa McDonald explores the obstacles and challenges that hold people back from leading happy, successful, and abundant lives. The show seeks to inspire and empower listeners to break the cycle of negative thoughts and actions that prevent them from reaching their goals. Each week, Lisa interviews newsmakers, entrepreneurs, motivational coaches, entertainers, athletes, philanthropists, activists and authors who embody what it is to "live fearlessly" and thrive. Guests and host share personal experiences and tips in frank, open discussion.

Phil R Mills

Phil R Mills is a dedicated husband and father, and a self-motivated and accomplished business professional, with extensive industry experience in the areas of *Leadership, Coaching, Business Management, Technology, Data Communications, Sales, and Personal Growth & Development*. Currently, he serves as a Sales Engineering Manager in the arena of Digital Communications focused on continued growth of his *Leadership and Technology* skills within his role of leading a team of Pre-Sales Engineers in the daily activities of supporting a Regional Sales office.

Phil has a proven track record of setting goals and achieving them; as he holds two master's degrees: one in *Business Administration* and one in *Project Management*. In addition, he is a licensed Insurance Agent, and currently is both a Certified John Maxwell Team Coach and a Certified Dave Ramsey Master Financial Coach. In his spare time, Phil is using his *Talents, Knowledge, Experience, and Wisdom* in Entrepreneurial endeavors of providing value to others through public speaking engagements and coaching services, in which he has developed a highly structured and thriving Success Awareness Coaching Program.

As part of his extracurricular activities in *Coaching, Public Speaking, Teaching and Writing*; Phil is incorporating key learnings and life lessons from personal experience and failures, to help others in their own personal journey of self-discovery, personal growth and development, financial planning, and goal achievement.

Stay tuned, as Phil has many "*irons in the fire*" and there is guaranteed future work and offerings to be on the lookout for!

The Power of Tent Making

By Phil R. Mills

In society today, it is quite common to find that most individuals are working a job or in a career that was the result of a chosen path that was easiest, had the least resistance, looked the most glamorous or highest paying at the time, or part of a chosen educational and career choice dictated or sold to them as being in their best interest.

In speaking to youth and young adults, it is an eye opening experience for them when I share and communicate the facts and statistics regarding how common it is for students to not have a chosen career path or major prior to college, and to change major's multiple times during college, and then to ultimately end up in a career or job that really has nothing to do with the degree earned. These statistics reflect the fact that it is very rare for young adults to know exactly who they are, what they want to do, and who they want to become, and to already be down a path in thought, planning, and action. Thus, it's really a matter of trial and error and evolving forces that leads them into the ultimate wage-earning job and career.

As part of my Success Awareness Coaching activities with adults; it is commonplace to hear that they are working a job or career that does not bring happiness and fulfillment, and feels more like being in a prison, in which the walls keep closing in as each day, month, and year passes. Many overcome this by taking on job change after job change, but not in a manner that has walked them through a process of structured self-analysis and life-planning. In general, most folks are functioning in the state of "insanity" - *doing the same thing over and over and expecting different results*.

This functioning state of being an employee to an organization and getting paid for doing a specific job or task, at an agreed upon hourly rate or salary, is a form of being a slave to time and money as an "*Indentured Servant*", in which one gets paid some form of compensation in exchange for their time. Typically, wages are paid out by the hour served. Therefore, to increase the amount of compensation, one must either <u>work more hours</u> or <u>increase the value</u> they are able to provide within the hours of service given. The desire to increase value is why there is an education industry estimated to be valued at more than a 2,000-Billion-dollar market within the next 5-7 years. Unfortunately, the time used up for existing job, family, friends, life hobbies, and sleep seems to limit and make it almost impossible for many to pursue higher education.

Congratulations! If you are reading this chapter, you are not the norm, but in what I consider to be the upper percentile of those with strong desire and supporting effort to capitalize on the limited resource labeled as TIME. This chapter is not about time management methods, but instead, it is focused on delivering thought awareness and understanding to current circumstances and available options for consideration and pursuit of making positive change in a functioning manner.

It is at this point I must reflect on one of the many great quotes I ever received and often think about from the great Jim Rohn…

> *"You don't get paid for the hour. You get paid for the <u>value</u> you bring to the hour."*

Upon first hearing and receiving this quote, I was sure it was all about the "hourly wage". However, after much thought and examination of life's experiences, I quickly determined that this simple quote is about <u>everything</u> in life that we devote our time to. In such reflection, I quickly concluded that in order to better myself, I must work to bring <u>more value</u> in EVERYTHING I do and also capitalize on the time given to do such things. Then to expand that thought, the things that are done to bring more value must be <u>focused on others!</u> Such valued service must help others deal with pain, problems, challenges, etc… In doing this, as it is written in the GREAT BOOK, the reward and riches will come tenfold.

It is at this point, one will wonder how they can provide additional value to generate more income, and two possible solutions of thought are commonly considered:

> Solution 1) How and what can I do to supplement my current job and income?
>
> or
>
> Solution 2) How do I get paid more at the job I'm at?

In looking to assess and answer these questions, it is my belief that one must become an entrepreneur at some level.

In the marketplace today, the word "Entrepreneur" is a sexy glamour buzzword, in which many individuals are attempting to be one in some shape or form.

If you take the time to research the different definitions that are out there for the meaning of the word "Entrepreneur", you will find two common keywords: _business_ and _risk_. The dedicated and focused entrepreneur is someone that will take on the highest risk to pursue the achievement of a determined business desire or goal. When it says "_highest risk_" it means you are willing to sacrifice many of life's joys and pleasures while also willing to risk losing EVERYTHING! – Now that is true "Entrepreneurship".

Truth be told, many do not really desire to be an entrepreneur, but do want to find an answer to generating more income; and in this pursuit, most will either take on additional _"Indentured Servant"_ work in the form of a 2nd job (Solution #1) or will strive to get higher pay in the current job by either the pursuit of a promotion or growing skills via education (Solution #2). I will argue that striving for the promotion or higher education will require a form of entrepreneurship, known as "Intrapreneurship". This is when an employee takes on the entrepreneurship roles of ownership and problem solving in a manner of being self-inspired, self-motivated, and self-managed. These qualities can accomplish great things!

Gmail is one example of a famous product that was birthed from such Intrapreneurial spirit, in which an "employee" came up with the idea during "free time" that Google gives all its team members.

Beyond the typical employee, and the few inspired intrapreneurs, there are many others that have a higher desire and calling to become their own boss and successful "Entrepreneur".

For those want-to-be entrepreneurs, it's time to face the music...

The reality is, most of us who have the desire to be an "Entrepreneur" or claim we are one, really have not sacrificed or shown we are willing to take on the full risk required. Typically, most of us still have a day job and dream of getting our entrepreneurship activities to a point of allowing us the freedom to leave the 9-5 grind. Some are closer to being a true entrepreneur by taking the leap of "Blind Faith" and believing they will acquire their "wings" on the way down from the free fall of diving in headfirst. Unfortunately, many of these fledglings find themselves in need of going back to the 9-5 grind in order to pay the bills. Then there are those that have had a clear vision from a very early age, planned intently, utilized discerning forethought, had patience, practiced persistence, and failed forward to near perfection. This chapter is not for the latter group, but is written for those of us that dream of being the successful entrepreneur and one day being our own boss without being tied down to the corporate life or what some call a J.O.B.

For most, it is not an option to just quit one's current job or career and pursue one's personal passion and purpose, due to the financial needs of providing for self, family, and others. This is when it is of great value to understand the power of *"Tent Making"*.

When I was introduced to the concept and understanding of *"Tent Making"*, I was told a story about a man named Paul, who was a tent maker by day, and a man of purpose in all of his other waking hours. Paul had a life changing experience and vision that gave him a personal belief system that was driven to share a special message with all human beings. The only problem was, Paul's work in delivering this message provided no means of being able to provide food and clothing. Within this dilemma, Paul also found himself of value as a tent maker, in which such profession provided Paul compensation and a means to provide for himself and anyone needing assistance. In addition, Paul was able to keep focus on his driven purpose and message when not at his tent making job, and then over time, Paul also discovered he was actually able to share his message within parts of his tent making activities. Most importantly, Paul realized the value that his tent making job provided and he went at it every day with the highest level of enthusiasm and gratification so as to be a great tent maker. This resulted in Paul having security in his tent making job with all the availability to pursue his personal purpose and passion as desired.

Upon hearing this story; I had to immediately go out to the Internet and search about "tent making". To my surprise, the search results were all about Religion and Christianity, and at first, I was feeling a little duped. I knew that the person who shared this story was not trying to drive a message of Religion into me but was challenging me to understand the meaning of *"Tent Making"* specific to my attitude around my existing job and career. It was in this thinking that I kept an open mind and continued to read the articles and writings about tent making. In such, I discovered that there actually was a man named "Paul" who was both a disciple of Jesus Christ and a tent maker. Paul used the tent making profession to provide for himself while he was entirely focused on his ministry of spreading the word of Christ. What is interesting, is how this concept can ultimately be incorporated into current times and speak to those that feel stuck and unhappy in their career and jobs, because it's all about attitude and how you look at the benefit and value that the current job provides.

It reminds me of a story that the late great Zig Ziglar used to share about a lady who came up to him full of anger, complaining about how she hated her job and how mean the other employees were at that job. Zig's response to the lady was that her problems were about to get worse because he was pretty sure she was soon to be fired, based on her current attitude. At this point, the lady realizes that she might actually lose her job and told Zig she would do anything to change this situation. Zig worked to coach and assist the lady in identifying and writing down those things of value that her job provided. The list contained such things as: a higher than average paycheck, paid vacation, retirement, profit sharing, health and life insurance, training, private office and parking space. The lady was then instructed to look in the mirror every morning and every night and say that she loves her job for each of the reasons on the list. Six weeks later, Zig saw the lady again and she communicated how great the job was doing and she couldn't believe how much the people at the job had changed! The interesting fact was, the only actual change that had happened, was in the lady's attitude and how she viewed and approached her job.

This method of using newly acquired *"mental floss"* in replacing the *"stinking thinking"* with *"an attitude of gratitude"* for all the value provided by the existing career and job is the hidden secret and power of tent making. Within the tent making job, one is provided many benefits while having the flexibility to also pursue their passion and purpose.

I have found that once one understands the value of the tent making job and its purpose of filling a need in supporting a successful entrepreneurship transition; there is opportunity to utilize both the career job (tent making) and the entrepreneurship endeavor in a way that they can feed on each other and actually generate growth in each. This is where the *"flywheel"* power of a tent making job working in conjunction with an entrepreneurial effort kicks in! The important piece and challenge is to assess and ensure you can be in a career or job that supports and complements the entrepreneurial goals and demands.

So how do we take our desire to be an entrepreneur and this knowledge around the power of tent making and put it into action with guaranteed success? One such proven formula for success is as follows:

Step 1: Have a documented "Purpose" with clearly defined Vision, Mission, Values, and Goals.

If you don't have this in place, don't waste any further energy or time in the pursuit of some entrepreneurship venture, but instead seek out on a personal journey to complete this task. The quickest and best way is to seek out a highly qualified Mentor or Coach that focuses in the area of Success Awareness, Peak Performance, and/or Life skills. I strongly recommend that you find an individual that first works with you in the process of self-discovery and self-awareness, to be incorporated into the typical structure and content of success coaching. Unfortunately, most of the programs being provided in the market today; only focus on getting someone to identify their core values, beliefs, and associated desires, which then are used in the development of documented goals to be worked within a structured goal achievement program and process. However, most people always fall short in having the discipline and persistence of achieving the documented goals, and quickly find themselves right back where they started with the undesired bonus of lost time and money. In the journey of self-discovery and self-awareness, a good coach helps one discover and overcome the psychological barriers that ultimately hold one back from achieving any desired goals, happiness, and feeling of fulfillment. With the aid of a great coach, the self-discovery journey should bring an individual to a personal understanding of true talents, ambitions, and desires which ultimately serve as the source of one's personal passion and purpose.

Step 2: Point the Compass in the Right Direction and Build a Documented Plan.

Once you understand your true purpose and passion that gives personal fulfillment and happiness, it is now time to develop a plan to be incorporated into your life. Such a plan should provide a documented path in achieving the ability to devote your desired amount of time in delivering service to others while fulfilling your defined *"Happiness Map"*.

Here are some additional quotes that I revisit often:

"If one strives to achieve a goal with no plan; they are only dreaming."

"If you don't design your own life plan, chances are you'll fall into someone else's plan. And guess what they have planned for you? – Not much!" – Jim Rohn

It is in the development of the plan that you will determine if there is need for a *"Tent Making"* job, and if so, you will determine if your current job fits the requirements or if you may need to look for a different one that ultimately supports and compliments the demands of your desired entrepreneurship endeavors.

Such a plan should include:

- Your documented Vision, Mission, and Values supporting your WHY;
- Goals that are clearly defined, quantifiable, and having deadlines for achievement;
- Requirements incorporated into the defined goals specific to needed supplies/tools, time, and money (capital);
- Achievement Timeline based on prioritized goals;
- Checkpoints and Milestones.

Building a Plan = Preparation … so remember:

"The Key to any Success is in the Preparation!!!"

Step 3: Work the Plan

Now that you have a well-documented plan with goals defined and prioritized with desired completion dates, it is time to work the plan in achieving these goals. In this step there are three words of wisdom:

1) ACTION – It is in action that work is completed, and achievement is made. Action reduces fear and increases courage. Without action, there is no movement, no progress, no growth and absolutely *NO SUCCESS.*

2) PERSISTENCE – With persistence will come great success; as persistence is the direct result of habit. Those who have cultivated the HABIT of persistence seem to enjoy insurance against failure. If there is lack of persistence, the ability for it to be conquered will depend entirely upon one's INTENSITY of DESIRE. Without persistence, you will be defeated, even before you start. With persistence, you will win. There is no substitute for *PERSISTENCE!*

3) PATIENCE – One must have patience in the journey and the time it will take to get to the desired arrival point in which the entrepreneurial activities are able to become an individual's full-time profession. Many abandon and miss out on the rewards of achievable goals, due to impatience.

Step 4: Track, Measure, Assess, and Adjust

It is imperative to be able to always know how you are tracking to your plan, as this provides a mechanism in supporting both discipline and motivation. It is at this step you want to schedule regular goal reviews recommended to be completed at least Daily, Weekly, Quarterly, and

Annually. In performing such reviews, one should document and assess current status relative to planned checkpoint and milestone targets. In assessing, use this as an opportunity to adjust and fine-tune your plan as you are actively working it and making forward movement and momentum. The desired outcome of this step is to be able to validate the documented plan, assess progress, adjust as needed, and keep forward momentum.

Step 5: Live and Be Happy!

If you have gotten to this step after working steps 1 through 4, you should be living a life of happiness and fulfillment because you are filled with hope and living to your passion and purpose either part-time or full-time. Success or failure at this point really doesn't matter, as you are living a life of providing value to self and others to a clearly defined passion and purpose that can only result in personal happiness and fulfillment, that many search for, but never find.

I hope that you may find your "Superpower" in both tent making and entrepreneurship while ultimately finding self, true happiness, and fulfillment in just living and enjoying the many blessings of life!

***

Phil R Mills

https://philrmills.com

https://prmstudios.com

https://www.linkedin.com/in/philrmills

pmills@prmstudios.com

(816) 379-6471

Hallie Bigliardi

Hallie Bigliardi is the published author of *Take Back the Reins – The Truth About Why You're Stuck and How to Get Moving Again*. With the help of horses, Hallie facilitates and coaches individual Equine Guided Education (EGE) sessions and group workshops. Using her uniquely integrated approach, which honors the interconnected aspects of body, mind, spirit, and soul, Hallie helps clients address the challenges we all face in the process of human development and life.

Hallie is a SkyHorseEGE™ certified coach and instructor. Under the mentorship of Ariana Strozzi Mazzucchi, founder of SkyHorseEGE™, Hallie spent eight years developing her skills as a facilitator and coach by staffing and teaching for SkyHorseEGE™ programs and helping to certify hundreds of people from all over the world in the work of Equine Guided Education.

Drawing from her extensive study of human development themes through the lens of archetypes and intuitive-archetypal astrology, Hallie bridges the practices of semantics and the body-mind-spirit concept with the themes and language of the soul. An expert in the areas of relationships, leadership, authentic communication, and facilitating transformational breakthroughs, Hallie has developed a unique and effective approach for getting unstuck and moving forward toward meaningful change.

Entrepreneur on Purpose

By Hallie Bigliardi

When traveling in a new town, the first thing I want is a map. I want guidance to understand where I am in relation to points of interest, the market, a meeting place, an historical site, so I know what direction I need to go to reach my desired location. Usually, the first map I come across is the free map given to me by the hotel or the rental car company. You know what I'm talking about, right? These maps are free because they are sponsored by specific businesses and attractions. The sponsor's locations are highlighted by large icons, the maps are not to scale, and they don't include all the streets or street names.

What happens when I use these maps? I walk out of my hotel following the map, and pretty soon, I find myself at a crossroads that is not on the map, and I have to decide which way to go. Choosing the wrong street can take me further into unmarked territory. At this point, I find myself needing to trust my own sense of direction.

Writing my first book was similar, as was starting my business. I sought out guidance from mentors who have been successful. I read "how to" books and took classes to learn the skills and strategies I thought would help me be successful. The things I learned were helpful. . . to a point. As an entrepreneur, there comes a point where no one else can tell you which way to go or which decision will yield the desired result. It's up to YOU.

Internal Guidance System

When these moments arise, how do you know what choice to make? How do you decide? There is wisdom inside of you, and this part of you knows the answer. It is your internal guidance system.

You were born with an internal guidance system. This system includes resources that are hard-wired at birth, your internal compass, and other aspects that develop as you grow and experience life. Your body, mind, spirit, and soul all have components connected to your internal guidance system, and integration of these aspects is imperative for peak performance. A lack of integration of any one aspect will impair your system's function.

Your internal compass is your soul, including both the personal and impersonal (eternal) aspects, and certain elements of your intuition. It is the principle component of your internal guidance system. It holds the coordinates of your highest potential, and it is always directing you toward them.

The aspects of your internal guidance system that can be developed include somatic awareness and cognitive functions such as imagination, memory, reasoning, and intuition. Attunement to your internal guidance system goes hand in hand with a healthy self-esteem, which includes the capacity for self-responsibility and trusting yourself.

As with any system, if one element gets out of alignment or disconnected, the system cannot function properly, and outcomes will not be optimal. If you are having trouble making a change or a significant decision, and it has led to feeling stuck, consider it like a warning light on your dashboard signaling that there's a breakdown in your internal guidance system.

Inevitably, we experience conflicts and challenges in life that cause us to pull back or withdraw, and in so doing we diminish, restrict, or retract the energy that flows through our body. For example, experiencing the break-up of a relationship or a failed business venture can cause an initial reaction of pulling back to isolate yourself and a withholding or stuffing of your feelings and emotions. This energetic contraction is a normal response to conflict and the pain you would prefer to avoid, and it may take some time to process your feelings, which is also normal. As long as you move through the process, eventually allowing your energy and emotions to flow, and you re-engage in life, your system will return to balance.

However, if the contraction of energy is held over time because you continue to withhold your feelings and energetic expression, you will begin to drift out of alignment with your internal compass. The unresolved energetic block causes dis-ease in your system, and this blocked energy can manifest as an emotional disorder or a physical disease. The flow of your life force and energy is linked to your emotional and physical well-being, and this highlights the importance of addressing the problems that cause energetic blocks and restrictions. Unaddressed energetic constrictions can become deep and debilitating, cutting you off from your internal guidance system.

Your entire being seeks alignment, so when there is a disconnect your spirit goes to work to bring it to your attention. It wants you to find the block or the breakdown, to acknowledge it, and grow through it, allowing the experience to be integrated, and alignment to be restored. If you do not heed the messages from your internal guidance system, you may start to experience a breakdown in your external environment. This can show up as financial hardship, relationship difficulties, physical illness, or some type of crisis. The more you ignore or resist, the more difficult your situation can become as your spirit turns up the volume to get your attention.

Balance and alignment can be restored. Through awareness you can begin to recognize the patterns and perceptions you have developed as a result of blocked emotions and feelings, and by releasing what's been blocked, your energy will begin to flow, allowing you to change unproductive patterns and shift your perspective. You will regain the sensitivities that connect you to your internal guidance system, leading to the clarity of purpose and flow that contribute to satisfaction.

Clarity of Purpose

As an entrepreneur, it is important to have clarity of direction and purpose in order to lead your business forward toward success. It is also important to define what success means to you. If you strive toward someone else's definition of success, you might find that the success you achieve does not bring satisfaction. If you achieve a goal or realize a desired outcome, and you do not feel satisfied, this is an indication that your goal or desired outcome was not in alignment with your core values and your soul's purpose. In order for you to feel successful and satisfied your business must be connected to your soul's desire, and your way of doing business must be in alignment with your core values and your soul's purpose.

We are individuals *and* we are part of a whole—the whole of humanity. Just as each grain of sand makes up the beach and each drop of water makes up the ocean. All is one. This seems like a simple concept, and yet, it can be difficult for our finite minds to comprehend.

While brief in the timeline of all humanity, your individual journey matters. Your existence matters, and there is a purpose for you being alive at this time. The desire to be an entrepreneur is not just about making money for yourself; it's about bringing something forward that the world needs, a new or improved service or product; it's about making a difference in the lives of people, animals, and/or the environment (the natural world).

Early in my career, I was introduced to the ideas of Martha Graham and her philosophy on life and purpose. She believed, as I do, that the energy that runs through us is our life force, and that energy is uniquely expressed by and through each individual. None of us is exactly the same. The full authentic expression of this uniqueness is our gift to the world. If we hold back our expression, it will be lost, missing from the world. Our responsibility is to allow our expression to flow by keeping the channel to our internal guidance system open.

Keeping the channel open means we do not allow our energy to become blocked or stuck, and if it does, we are tasked with finding a way to break free, to get our energy flowing again. I am convinced that blocked or stuck energy is the underlying cause for the majority of what ails us, including physical diseases and emotional disorders. Our health and our vitality have a direct relationship with how we manage our energy and how we relate to our life's purpose.

In 2010, I began to diligently study the concept of "life's purpose," which is also referred to as our "calling" or "God's will." It started with the urge I had to discover my own life's purpose and continued as I saw how integral it seemed to understanding the human condition and to finding ways to assist my clients toward their own breakthroughs. It seemed like the quintessential puzzle piece necessary to have a satisfying life and to navigate change and transition. I became somewhat obsessed with it. I read many books on the topic that offered a variety of strategies and methods to help one discover life's purpose.

For years, I believed the search for my life's purpose led me to an Equine Guided Education program, where I discovered my purpose was to be an EGE coach and facilitator. You would have read similar words on my website. Much of what I'd read and studied, up to that point, seemed to support the idea that each of us has "a" purpose—as in a singular purpose, one main purpose, *uno*, the one thing, the "*it*".

But then my perspective on the concept of life's purpose began to change. Inspired by the book *Designing Your Life* by Bill Burnett and Dave Evans, I started to see multiple potential outcomes when applying design principles to planning one's future, all of which were exciting and desirable and "on purpose." There was no singular purpose. One's gifts, talents, and interests could be channeled into a myriad of different goals and activities. Their examples demonstrated the importance of being connected to the *why* behind a goal or activity and showed that not all goals and activities that one engages in need to have the same *why* or purpose.

As this idea of multiple potential outcomes permeated my thoughts, I began to see the pitfall of my previous philosophy around purpose. I felt the rigidity of the idea that we should have a singular purpose. In the midst of this contemplation, I came across something I'd written a few years before as part of a homework assignment. We were asked to write some belief statements about who we are, our goals, and our purpose.

I began to read it.

"God created me for *a* purpose. Each person is created for *a* purpose . . ."

The emphasis on the singular purpose made me cringe, and I was so repulsed, I couldn't even read the rest of it. It was strange to remember the inspiration and connection I'd felt to those words as I wrote them, and then to feel the repulsion to those same words as I read them in that moment.

So, what changed?

At the time I read that document, I was not practicing EGE. I was on sabbatical from my work. The role I had played for several years had come to completion, and I had decided to take some time off before making any decision about how to move forward. According to what I had written, if I was not practicing EGE, then I was off my purpose. But that didn't feel right to me. I was taking a sabbatical "on purpose." I wanted to give myself the time and space to imagine the future without any lingering expectations based on the work I had been doing. What if I decided to pursue something new? What if I decided not to continue doing EGE? Who would I be if I weren't practicing EGE? According to this document, I wouldn't be me. But I absolutely knew that was not true.

Redefining my belief about purpose caused me to review an old contributor, the concept of "God's will." My view on this had also evolved over the years. When I was a little girl in church there was no greater calling than to be a missionary. Missionaries were revered for their commitment and sacrifice. The church would hold prayer meetings where people would pray for each other to have the will of God revealed. On more than one occasion, I remember being terrified that God would call me to be a missionary, or some other thing that I would dread. Back then I didn't know that God's will would never be something I would dread. I didn't understand, as I do now that the things I love, the things that inspire me, and the things I'm drawn to are there because that is how I was created. These things are of my soul, and they are the guideposts of my purpose.

During my process of redefining my belief about "life's purpose," I listened to a talk by Thomas Hübl, a spiritual teacher. He asked questions like *How vital do we feel? How is our life energy?* He helped me understand that if we get to the end of our day and we feel depleted, we need to examine where we were holding back, where we've dissociated, where our energy was blocked. The goal is to create an awake and present life by working on the unconscious areas and moments (where our energy gets blocked) in order to illuminate and address them (so we keep the channel open). **This is our life's purpose.**

If we need a holiday to recharge ourselves, something in our life is not working. We need to examine where we are not living our life's purpose because we are allowing our energy to be blocked/stuck, creating friction, resistance, and lowering our vitality. The more we step into our life's purpose (allowing our unique expression to flow), the more we will feel recharged by what we do.

My purpose is to be fully me, and your purpose is to be fully you, not what society or our families think we *should* be. If I don't do me, and you don't do you, then the world is missing something it is meant to have. We each have our own natural rhythm and energetic expression, and our purpose is to keep our energy flowing and expressing. The underlying, energetic basics are the same for everyone, but this will translate into action differently for each person, and there are multiple ways for each of us to fulfill our purpose.

Fate and Destiny

When we talk about purpose, the concepts of fate and destiny are not far behind. As I have just spoken about multiple possibilities and potential outcomes for your life, I want to clarify that I'm not saying there are infinite possibilities. The concept of infinite possibility is popular, and I see it being touted by some influential teachers and speakers. This idea is popular in the United States as we call ourselves "the land of possibility," and it gets reinforced by the "rags to riches" stories that we love to hear or read about.

The cosmic universe may contain the potential for infinite possibility, but our individual lives do not. In our lifetime, we do not have infinite possibilities, but in most cases, we have more possibilities and opportunities than we realize or acknowledge as we move toward our destiny. Our purpose is to pursue our destiny to its fullest within the boundaries of our fate.

What is fate? Fate has many facets. Fate is the culture and the time in history in which you were born. Fate is your parents, your family, your DNA.

Fate in our DNA goes like this. Robert began gymnastics at a young age, and he was great at it. He was athletic and flexible and had excellent balance. He was on the path to Olympic level competition until he grew too tall. Fate is Robert surpassing the maximum height at which a gymnast can compete at the Olympic level. Robert's fate of not being able to pursue Olympic competition created a boundary that helped direct him toward his destiny of becoming a teacher, speaker, and author.

The generations that came before influence the range of possibility that exists now for certain things connected to social and cultural consciousness. We can see fate's influence at the social and cultural levels through the success of Oprah Winfrey. Oprah's potential to be who she is came about because of the groundwork set by Martin Luther King, Jr., among others, and the movement he championed. If Oprah had been born prior to this movement, the possibility for her to develop into the person she is today would not have existed. The social changes we are making today will influence the fate and the potential of generations to come.

Time is also an element of fate. Gestation, germination, and lifespan are elements of fate, and we won't get far by fighting fate or feeling victimized by it. It is through the choices we make based on what is fated that we have the power to co-create our destiny, the highest potential for our life.

Fate often has negative connotations. We see fate as restrictive or something bad that happens because it wasn't what we were hoping for in the moment. But it's really all about perspective. A failed business venture may feel disappointing, but it may also have kept you from continuing to pursue something that would not have brought true satisfaction. In some cases, after time has passed, we can reflect and see the bigger picture, and in it we can see how fate was working for us, and how fate contributed to something we now appreciate or even cherish because it directed us toward our soul's purpose and the fulfillment of our destiny.

***

To Contact Hallie:

Telephone 1-408-859-9660

hallie@halliebigliardi.com

www.halliebigliardi.com

Sonia Novick

Hello! My name is Sonia Novick. I am an entrepreneur, motivational coach, certified NLP Practitioner, and "Curandera – Healing Coach." I have a secret entrepreneurial formula my dad passed on to me that allows most entrepreneurs to earn millions of dollars and avoid common mistakes!

My goal is to meet the demand of those desiring to learn these entrepreneurial secrets—including better health alternatives, enhanced food and wellness products by re-education of lifestyle diet, and emotional/mental reprogramming changes. Offering proven and verifiable life-changing entrepreneurial formulas, my health coaching strategies help your body and mind to work efficiently, celebrating and enhancing life instead of confusing and unbalancing the body, mind, and spirit…

Besides being an entrepreneur, I am a Certified Health Coach, a health supplement formulator, and the inventor of a whole superfood product that stimulates your immune system and activates an immune-compromised system back to optimal health. This invention/formulation alone makes millions of dollars and helps health researchers, health practitioners, scientists, virologists, and millions of auto-immune compromised people all over the world to improve their healing process completely and naturally from cancer and other issues.

Learn how to get rid of brain fog and activate your mind for achieving success with total health and wellness in living an A-Bun-Dace life!

Self-Made Multi-Millionaire Entrepreneurial Secret Formula

By Sonia Novick

Hello! My name is Sonia Novick. I am going to share an entrepreneurial formula my dad used all his life to earn millions and avoid common mistakes made by most entrepreneurs. When I was in my early twenties, I always looked up to my dad for his amazing business skill-set and how he would reinvent himself in a myriad of different ways with his businesses. He had the Midas Touch, as I have as well. Following my father's advice and his success formulas, I have learned the following: being the source of products is key to controlling your venture. As he stated, "Sell the distribution end of your business, but keep the sourcing or product manufacturing end of it, and you will always have an income."

My father is who inspired me to be an entrepreneur my entire adult life. He was a self-made millionaire by the time he was in his 30's, as he became the co-owner of Lafayette Radio Electronics (which later became Radio Shack); until he sold it and moved to Mexico in 1950. He started a venture in 1955 called Pilas Aguila Negra—in English, Black Eagle Batteries Manufacturing Plant—in Mexico City.

In 1959, he went to Germany to learn about an advanced battery technology, gaining the secrets of their technology from this outfit. He implemented it and improved the technology with his battery factory; these batteries were longer-lasting than any other battery in the marketplace. Since my father improved upon the Germans' technology to the point that the quality of his batteries was far superior to the German mfg.'s batteries, this German mfg. outfit ended up buying out the battery company in 1965 for millions of dollars. Shortly after, in the late summer of 1965, he co-founded a company that made Cold Rolled Steel, called "Cold Rolled De Mexico" until he passed away in 1986.

If anyone is responsible for the fervor in me to be a successful entrepreneur by doing what I have a passion for and profound knowledge of, it's my dad. Being a self-made millionaire is a goal toward which my dad gave me the formulas to achieve. My credit is achieved in making the persistent effort to arrive at this juncture.

I want to share this formula with you, if you truly want to be a successful entrepreneur. The following success steps are the very ones my dad passed on to me:

- Get into a business you have great knowledge in and experience doing.

- Have great passion for the business you are going to start your enterprise in.

- Find a niche in a vertical market.

- Develop your proprietary products or services.

- Become the source of these product(s) or services and you will never have to worry about not being successful or not having an income stream.

- In other words, when you control the product(s) that are in demand, you now have a solid foundation to build your business abundantly and effortlessly.

- Give the world the product or service they need the most, and you will always be financially successful and secure.

- Have a business ownership mentality with good financial management skills, NOT an employee mentality.

- Take responsibility for all aspects of the business and work long hours when necessary, depending on the demands of the venture.

- Manage the growth of your venture; sub out to other business outfits that can service the different aspects of your venture in order to grow your business into a multi-million-dollar outfit.

- Put all you have into it: i.e. your blood, sweat, tears, and passion, and when needed, get advice from successful friends in the industry.

- Most startup owners work harder and longer than any of their employees for two reasons: 1) It's their passion and joy to have a successful outcome, and 2) They love what they do for a living, so it does not seem like work.

- Invest in your expertise; any surplus of cash that comes from your venture, reinvest it back into your venture. Do not invest your surplus in so-called 'financial opportunities' you're not knowledgeable about. Stick with what you know.

- Start your enterprise(s) on a small scale, and as you build it, keep reinvesting extra cash in doing PR campaigns, digital marketing, etc.

- Keep working until your venture is a multi-million-dollar outfit, then sell the distribution end once you have a great offer.

- You must have grit, perseverance, and determination to succeed in whatever entrepreneurial venture you take on.

- Learn from previous failures; so called failures are nothing more than expensive lessons. This is what I call the school of hard knocks. The best schooling I've ever received was through loss; the pain helped me to not repeat the same mistakes again.

- If you're going to partner up in a 50/50% venture, make sure your partner has the same drive you do to make the endeavor successful.

- Make sure you have a partnership contract in writing, so everyone remembers exactly what was agreed to.

- Do several JVs (Joint Ventures) that benefit both parties in the same vertical markets.

- You will have good days and bad days; hang in there, and when the tough gets tougher, bootstrap it and look for opportunities to increase or expand the revenue of your business.

- Most millionaires or billionaires have made it, lost it, and made it again. It's all part and parcel of the entrepreneurial learning cycle and journey.

I have owned a water filtration manufacturing company, a gem and mineral retail business, a shareware delivery distributions company, and a successful venture capital brokerage in the telecom project financing industry. I really honed my public speaking and mentoring skills in Las Vegas, NV, continuing this trend for the past 11 years. Getting my Life Coaching certification, I worked on several coaching website portals online. I have helped over 20,000 people change their lives for the better. In 2011, I started Living Technologies, a Super Food company which has exponentially grown since. It has evolved into a superfood apothecary for people who have auto immune compromised conditions such as cancer. This venture is where my expertise and genius truly shine. I am an innate formulator of superfood substances and supplements, a master at healing and detoxing the body with my proprietary protocols that help heal the human body from so many diseases. I have created and formulated my own proprietary healing superfood kits, which assists in healing cancer naturally, as well as many other auto-immune compromising diseases.

In my 44 years of business experience and acumen, I have followed my father's success steps. I have had enterprises that made millions. I have also lost money learning my craft. I have also made millions in my solo business ventures. All these experiences have taught me how to be more like my dad.

Now, I have a Superfood and Health Coaching venture where I get hired to help heal people who have immune compromised diseases, incorporating my Whole-Food store to offer the proper nutritional support for those seeking healing and lifestyle changes. I have studied the cause of disease, as well as alternative healing modalities on how to live a healthy lifestyle, for over 40 years. As Tony Robbins stated, "Live by example and be the example". I pride myself on having found healthy, natural alternative solutions to staying healthy and vibrant in order to have a pain-free body and being able to extend my telomeres and lifespan.

Here is a list of diseases my inventions are helping:

- Cancer
- Autoimmune diseases
- Autism Spectrum Disorders (ASD)
- Epstein-Barr Virus (EBV)
- Hepatitis B virus (HBV)
- Herpes Simplex virus (HSV)
- Cystitis
- Hepatitis C virus (HCV)
- Multiple sclerosis (MS)
- Urinary tract infection (UTI)
- Rheumatoid arthritis (RA)
- Endometriosis
- Chronic Fatigue Syndrome (CFS)
- IgA deficiency disorder
- Myalgic Encephalomyelitis (ME)
- Mycobacteria infections
- Parkinson's disease
- Tuberculosis
- Fibromyalgia
- Human papillomavirus (HPV)
- Lupus (Systemic lupus erythematosus, SLE)
- HIV AIDS
- Dengue fever
- Pneumonia infection

- Warts caused by viral infection

- Norovirus

- Malaria Influenza virus (flu)

- Herpes simplex virus (HSV)

- Q fever (Coxiella burnetii)

- Polycystic ovary syndrome (PCOS)

- Chicken pox (varicella zoster virus)

- Psoriasis

- Respiratory tract infections

- Ulcerative colitis, Crohn's disease

- Type 1 diabetes (T1DM), insulin-dependent diabetes (IDDM)

- Type 1.5 diabetes, Latent autoimmune diabetes of adults (LADA)

Due to my Immune Activator Kit invention, I have become an expert in the alternative healing field. I have assisted medical professionals like trained doctors, functional medicine doctors, virologists, scientists, alternative medicine doctors, chiropractors, naturopaths, acupuncture or Chinese medicine doctors, and others who come to me for advice regarding this kit. My health protocols help to greatly heal intestinal tract issues and other immune compromised issues billions of humans on the earth are now suffering with due to the destruction of our environment, compromised food, soil, and water sources. I am a recognized innovator and expert in the field of probiotic combinations. My inventions and products are helping to heal thousands, if not millions, of people around the world with everything from 4th stage pancreatic to other aggressive cancers.

My vast health coaching knowledge consists of how the body truly functions and what protocols are required to detoxify and heal the body from the inside out.

When educated consumers hire me to be their coach, they know that restored health will likely be the outcome. Your body has an amazing ability to heal itself. With the proper guidance from an expert, directing you on proper detoxification protocols and appropriate nutrients, you can naturally create the lifestyle change you are seeking. Your desire to achieve better health, without ever compromising your immune system or your pocketbook, can be fulfilled. I assist those who seek life giving remedial therapies and know experts, such as myself, exist in the field of natural health to successfully help people recover from immune compromised conditions into healthy living lifestyles. Bottom line, I have the utmost passion for what I do; thereby my various enterprises succeed.

You want to know what it takes to be an entrepreneurial success? This chapter has covered some of the details and keys to being successful in your life. No matter how large or small your successes, goals, or dreams are, they all add up. In the word of masters, "Take baby steps towards your venture, and your business goals will out-picture themselves into reality." These baby steps will lead you to a fruitfully amazing dreams achieving this with a vibrant life!

- When you overcome negative patterns in your thinking—that you're not good enough or nothing, which was instilled in you at an early age by your parents and peers who didn't know any better.

- Your baby steps lead you to your end goal.

- Another step towards ultimate success is to start dissolving those toxic beliefs within you about you being a failure. Remember, failure is how we learn not to make this mistake again; this is the lesson.

- Remember that behind every failure, you'll find the steps toward your success.

- Start practicing how to become a success and a money magnet NOW!

- There are so many amazing self-help books, such as this one, that help your mind to focus on what you wish to create into this physical realm instead of "miscreating"—a word I have coined. Stop miscreating negative experiences and outcomes in your world of experience.

- We all need to be hyper-aware of where and what we put our attention on, for this is what causes us to create the positive or negative outcomes in our lives.

We humans are literally manifestation machines! This is why it's so important to stop negative talk in our minds; have negative talk take a back seat and practice positive talk, being grateful for every baby step you take in creating your desired outcome. Gratitude and positive thinking are critical to succeeding with your business ventures. This is part and parcel for cracking the rich code for becoming a success in life.

The mantra I practice on a daily basis, or whenever I have angst about an outcome is:

HAVE NO EXPECTATIONS

STAY NEUTRAL

HAVE NO ATTCHMENT TO OUTCOME

I remind myself that the successful outcome of my venture is an inside job. Its literally in the invisible reality in my heart; I have already manifested it and am now in the process of out-picturing it in my future reality. Just like the Iris or Tulip flower sprouting from a bulb in the ground, you do not see it there until you plant it, feed it, then it out-pictures itself into form.

When I am not in "the Groove," or in sync with universal flow, regarding my projects or ventures, they slow down, or in some cases come to a halt. I can see clearly when I'm not in concert with universal flow, and instead in fear, resistance, lack, or limitation. This always blocks my flow and my good from appearing in my life; it keeps good things from manifesting into my life experience.

One thing I share with my coaching clients is that when we are out of alignment with this flow, things fall apart: we get sick, we fail to reach our goals, etc. So, I share with them what one of my coaches taught me: "You're either in scarcity = scare-city, or in abundance +

a-bun-dance." The block standing between the out-picturing of your dreams is that you're not in the flow due to being in scarcity and having unreasonable expectations that come from the EGO self. One of my other coaches shared this acronym with me: the word EGO:

Edging

God

Out

When you edge GOD out, then your genius is stifled, your EGO steps in and takes over, and most often causes chaos. When you invite your EGO to take a back seat and stop it from running amok in your ventures, you will be back on track towards creating an abundant life. Instead, you can invite your higher self to take the wheel and navigate your mind back into universal flow. When you follow this guidance, you will navigate your life into success.

With any business project, if you can imagine it in your mind's eye, you can create it into physical existence. Follow these steps to find yourself back in universal flow, manifesting effortlessly your desired outcomes, ventures etc. This is how we individually crack the Rich Code within ourselves.

- Realize there are no limitations except for the limiting beliefs we place on ourselves.

- Truly become uncorked and move into becoming a manifestation machine with a creative, high-octane engine.

- This is where mental discipline comes in.

- Focus on what you desire to create and leave the Doubting Thomas' behind, including your critical mind, your parents, your significant other, or any Doubting Thomas in your life.

- Liberate yourself from these limiting people, thoughts/beliefs and replace them with positive influences, re-framed belief systems, until you reach your desired outcome.

- This success game is all about reprogramming your mind for the attainment of success and giving yourself credit for all the baby-step successes you have accomplished in getting to your ultimate success apex.

- I never share my projects/ventures that are percolating in my inner world with any naysayers, or anyone at all.

- I hold my excitement and enthusiasm close to the vest as I see my project or venture unfolding and out-picturing itself into my desired outcome.

- Quantum Science has uncovered that the energy needed to manifest your project is in the solar plexus, so imagine holding this pressure cooker in the solar plexus which is growing and expanding with every passing day.

- While the pressure cooker is expanding within your invisible, intangible world, as this pressure grows, your desire to share it with others will also grow due to the exhilaration of seeing things coming together.

- But, you yourself will have to be super-disciplined not to verbally share any of these precious energies or developments with anyone until you have out-pictured your venture into physical reality.

There are some boundless mental tricks you can do in programming yourself for great success. I have manifested so many ventures here on this physical plane, and have done this with my manifestation formula bellow:

- I first visualize and imagine vividly what desired venture I want to create.

- I then go into great detail of visualization and imagine myself in a 3D movie already having attained this successful venture.

- Next, I feel and experience the out-picturing of this venture as already having happened. In the words of Tony Robbins, one of my mentors, "Act as if you already attained it." This means you feel it in your physiology as real.

- I DON'T SHARE my in-depth plan, or any details, with people verbally until it is out-pictured in the physical realms of reality. Remember, "Loose lips sink ships."

- As stated, before, do not let these manifesting energies dissipate by sharing the details with naysayers or others not involved in your project before it comes to fruition, or you will dissipate the built-up energies to manifest your project into reality.

- You need to think of placing your project into a sealed container in your body and build this energy and excitement within your being until your project out-pictures itself into reality.

- You need to imagine placing this project and all its components into a pressure cooker inside you to percolate in your invisible world until these energies become so intense and strong they have no option but to out-picture your venture into physical reality.

- Once you have realized your project, now go spill the beans—so to speak—and share it with the world to gain an even greater level of success!

I truly hope reading this chapter has enlightened, inspired, and enhanced your life. I encourage you to follow your dreams, to change your stars, and fortunes for only you can create the desired outcome you wish in your life, including attaining radiant health. This formula works for any age!

Wishing you optimal health in your life. "If you don't have your health, and are not enjoying a high quality of life, you have nothing." - Sonia Novick -

***

Sonia Novick

Your transformational health coach and mentor,

To contact Sonia:

You can learn more about my mentoring programs and our team on our website:

http://CancerFreeCoaching.com

If you have any more questions, feel free to email me at:
Sonia@CancerFreeCoachig.com

Gary Goodspeed

Gary Goodspeed attended Cumberland College in Williamsburg, KY where he majored in history. After college, he enlisted in the Air Force and spent the majority of his time at SAC Headquarters in Bellevue, NE.

His computer marketing career began in Denver, CO, and took him around the country, opening new offices for his employers.

Gary has multiple certifications in the field of hypnosis and is a graduate of both the Denver School of Hypnosis (1977) and Omni Hypnosis Training Center (2017) as a Certified Consulting Hypnotist. Gary's practice, TranceFormed Hypnosis, is located in Tryon, NC, where he resides with his wife, Vicky. He is a member of the National Guild of Hypnotists and is also a Certified Life Purpose Life Coach.

In addition to his hypnosis practice, Gary is a co-founder of The Open Road Alliance (the Alliance). The Alliance is a consortium of wellness practitioners sharing their specialties with the public through presentations and workshops. People can come and learn about the benefits of alternative wellness modalities like hypnosis, yoga, reiki, acupuncture, and more.

Gary and his wife, Vicky, are both musicians and regularly perform at different venues in-and-around Western North Carolina.

Never Too Late

By Gary Goodspeed

Hypnosis has fascinated me for as long as I can remember. From the moment I watched Bela Lugosi use his "preternatural" eyes acquire his next victim, I wanted to know more! What was this power he had, and can anyone do that? Could I do that? Even as a kid, I knew I was watching a fictional character in a movie, but still, there was a part of me that wanted to believe that this ability was real. Every time a vampire movie aired on Friday night's *Shock Theater*, hosted by Ghoulardi, I sat glued to our black-and-white TV, wholly captivated.

The Village of Lakemore, OH didn't have a town library, so my only resource was the small library in my elementary school. I can assure you back in the late 50s and early 60s the subject of hypnosis was not a common theme on those bookshelves. For the longest time, my only contact with hypnosis continued to be through movies, TV and occasionally comic books.

When I was in high school, my family moved to a bigger town, with a public library, in addition to the one at school. I made frequent visits to both locations and read whatever I could find about hypnosis. Because this topic was a little off the wall for my parents, I would secretly sneak in my reading when no one was around. It was not unusual to find me in the basement or lying on the top bunk of the bed getting in a chapter or two whenever I could. Fortunately, the resources that were now available to me were teaching me that hypnosis was a real process, and anyone could be a hypnotist.

With only my book smarts to guide me, I hypnotized my first two subjects at the ripe old age of eighteen. My initial trance experience was to command a teenage girl from the local high school to get down on all fours and bark like a dog; not my finest moment to be sure. My second opportunity came when a fellow student wanted to quit smoking. Although my method was not by the book, the trance was a success, and I felt a great sense of achievement. Armed with this experience, I continued practicing and studying hypnosis on my own, but I also needed to earn an income. As John Lennon quipped, "Life is what happens while you are busy making other plans." As I quickly learned, marriage and rent seem to happen when you least expect it.

My wife, Linda, and I were doing okay in our chosen careers, but we were not setting the world on fire. After much discussion, I convinced her to move to Boulder, CO to find fame and fortune. I chose Colorado because I spent time in Denver when I was in the Air Force. I always knew that I would want to go back someday. Colorado, at that time, was beginning to grow, but it was still a haven for new ways of thinking, including alternative methods of healing and wellness, as I would soon find out. It was here I located a bonafide school of hypnosis in Denver. So, with Linda's encouragement, I attended the school and received my first certification as a legitimate hypnotist. Now, what do I do with it?

When Linda and I moved to Colorado, neither of us had jobs waiting for us. Since Linda was a registered nurse, it did not take more than two interviews for her to secure employment. For me, it wasn't that easy. With our savings running low, we didn't have the resources for me to start a hypnosis practice, and I had to find employment. Although Denver was starting to grow, finding a choice marketing or sales position was taking more time than we hoped. I did eventually find what I considered a safe employment choice as a technician for TWX and Telex machines. This position eventually moved me into selling computers and software to large corporations and their customers. That decision started my long affiliation with the corporate world. Becoming a hypnotherapist was now put on indefinite hold.

Now don't get me wrong, there was a lot of good that came from working in the corporate world. My work moved me around the country from Ohio to Hawaii and back. I made great friends and experienced a diversity of cultures and cuisine. From Cajun cooking in Louisiana to drinking iced tea with pineapple instead of lemon in Hawaii, Linda and I enjoyed it all. Many of the moves we made were to establish new offices in new markets for my employer. Setting up shop in new cities takes a tremendous amount of effort and dedication. I did, however, finally discover that there was one person I could consistently help with hypnosis – me. During our tenure in Dallas, Tx, I began utilizing the effects of trance on myself. I used self-hypnosis to help me improve my marketing skills in a competitive computer world. The different trances included confidence, study skills, creativity, and public speaking. I had finally found a way to use my training, and it was for my betterment. However, a health issue from my past was about to resurface, and my treatment of choice, for some reason, was not hypnosis.

The decade of the 80s was a pivotal point in my life and my health. At the age of six, I started suffering from severe headaches. I remember all the tests conducted by doctors to determine the cause, but they were all inconclusive. The migraines dissipated during my teen and early adult years but came back with a vengeance while we were in Texas. Linda had access to some of the best doctors in the area, and so we began new test procedures. When the doctors couldn't find a cause for the pain, I followed the typical course of treatment, at the time, using muscle relaxers and opioids to manage the pain. I was not solving anything, but I could at least function and continue my career path.

By the late 90s and early 2000s, all hell broke loose: fibromyalgia and herniated lumbar discs now complicated my health concerns. Each caused havoc with my ability to function in daily life, personally and professionally. The pain I lived in made it impossible to work for a company outside the home. I began researching options on earning an income that gave me the freedom to work when I could and rest when I needed. Around that time, creating an online business and internet marketing were becoming the rage. With my background in computers, it seemed a natural fit for me to take advantage of the internet craze and start my own company.

A close friend and colleague, Ginny Dye, asked me to be a part of a new internet company she was developing: Together We Can Change the World (TWCCTW). Taking that position was the right solution for my health problems. I was able to control my work time and rest time, which allowed me to focus on a new concern - my wife's health was now faltering. Linda found a lump in her breast, leading to her first-round with breast cancer. She went through chemo and radiation, just like most of us would in those circumstances. It was tough watching her go through this stage of her life; the treatments took a tremendous toll on her.

Fortunately, Linda loved her work, which proved to be very therapeutic, but in 2008, her cancer returned. This occurrence resulted in even stronger drugs, taking even more out of her. To make matters worse, by 2010, Linda's mom could no longer live on her own and needed round the clock supervision. We decided to move into her home, where she had lived for seventy-plus years, instead of sending her to an assisted living center. Because Linda's work kept her going, and TWCCTW had closed its doors, I assumed the role of the primary caregiver. Our lives remained the same until five years later when, after nearly forty-two years together, Linda passed away doing battle with her third-round of cancer. The world as I knew it shattered before me, and for the first time in my life, I felt lost. As I continued to care for my mother-in-law, my life seemed to slow to a crawl. One day while listening to some music, one of Linda's favorite songs began playing. As it played, the music put me into an almost trance-like state, and memories filled my mind. I recalled something she shared with me before going to the hospital for the last time. She said, "I want you to promise me you will move on with your life. My brother can move in and take care of my mom. You need to find a life again." Although that was her desire, it took a few months before I could come to grips with what might lay ahead. Eventually, I decided I needed to take charge of the rest of my life, or the me I used to be would never be again.

To begin this new phase of my life, I moved to another part of town and started weaning myself off all the medications I was taking. My resolve was due in part to my health insurance company no longer covering the cost of one of my prescription. There was no way I could afford, on my own, the two-thousand-dollar monthly price tag. Although my doctor and I tried to find an alternative, nothing worked as well as the original medicine. I began to climb out of the fog produced by these medications; my mind cleared, and new thoughts and ideas flooded my brain with unique desires, wants, and goals. At least one old passion emerged with my latest thinking – the need to use hypnosis as part of my new wellness strategy. Just like my old routine back in Dallas, self-hypnosis, again, became a part of my daily activity. I utilized my training to modify my outlook and thinking, then added controlling my pain to the trances. I started believing in myself and realized I still had a life to live.

A year and a half later, at the age of sixty-six, I met Vicky Brooker, who was also recently widowed. We soon understood we had a significant role to play in the other's life. I was there to help her through the loss of her husband and the loss of their business. Vicky held fast the rudder on my new ship of discovery and helped me appreciate I had much more to give before I retired. We both had a desire for knowledge and moving forward. As I began sharing my life with Vicky, she watched the old me emerge, like a butterfly from a cocoon, and start taking charge of my surroundings. She unearthed things I had forgotten a couple of decades before: the man who pursued his dreams in the past was still there.

Vicky recognized within me a need to revitalize the talents that were once a natural part of me. She reawakened my passion for hypnosis in helping others, not just myself. I began this new life by going back to school and training for my second certification as a Consulting Hypnotist, also known as a Hypnotherapist. I started honing the skills of my past with the new tools taught today. I was like the proverbial kid in the candy store; I couldn't get enough. I took additional hypnosis classes focusing on specific needs and added to the arrows in my quiver. Before I opened my practice to the public, I took on my first two clients privately: Vicky and me. As I worked with Vicky, each session brought about profound changes for her; we were removing the negative grip of the past and present events that had shaken her life. She, too, was becoming a new person; she found the freedom to move forward and realize she also had so much more to give.

For me, the approach was "physician heal thyself." My mind and body adjusted to life without pharmaceuticals, but I was still living with the issues that caused me to be on all the medications in the first place. Self-hypnosis became my tool of choice as I continued my journey to wellness. To help others, I needed to become a product of my training. How else could I relate with the clients that would come through my door? It wasn't long before I was ready to hang out my shingle and start my new hypnosis practice. Like Dorothy from *The Wizard of Oz* found she always had the power to go home, I found I could manage my health. That revelation would take me beyond my hypnotherapy practice.

Not long after opening my door to the public, Vicky and I realized we needed a clean start to our new life together. For us, that meant moving someplace new to begin creating our memories and not be surrounded by the past. A few months later, we left Cincinnati, OH and moved to Tryon, NC. Western North Carolina proved to be a haven for alternative healing and thinking. I found a desire in me to seek new modalities that would facilitate and continue my wellness goals. Using yoga and ortho-bionomy proved a benefit to my body. It became apparent to Vicky, and I the need for others to experience what was happening in our lives.

To that end, we envisioned creating a community of healers and practitioners working together to demonstrate wellness is not just taking a pill; it requires our participation. We would accomplish this through monthly presentations and bi-monthly workshops demonstrating the different holistic modalities that are available. Our efforts have now culminated into The Healthy Path Initiative. As we grow and increase our base of healers, we hope to expand into all of North Carolina and beyond. Ultimately, our goal is to make holistic wellness an affordable alternative to all consumers.

I hope that my story, which focuses primarily on personal empowerment and reinvention, will benefit entrepreneurs of all stripes. However, for those of you who struggle with health or physical concerns, understand you do not have to operate at 100% every day to succeed in your new-found career. An important discovery for me was the realization that I could accomplish the goals I set forth while working within my physical limitations. When I started over, I was working with a fresh mind, but my body was still operating with its old nature. The first thing I did was learn how to get the most out of me physically, without exacerbating any existing problems that caused pain. For example, I couldn't sit at my computer for hours on end working, like I did when I was younger. So, I established a scheduled routine to change projects throughout the day; I had to learn to take breaks and allow my body to rest and recuperate as it continued to heal. Vicky calls this maintaining my energy level. Understanding that I have a certain amount of energy available each day, I set-up my routine based on what projects need the highest productivity.

I discovered I had to alter my lifestyle to build new strength and energy to meet the unique demands placed on me by my hypnotherapy practice. For example, enthusiasm is an admirable trait, but taking on too many clients in a day is not beneficial to the client, or me. I needed to take an active role in building my body through diet and exercise and physical therapy prescribed by my primary care physician. Utilizing my Silver Sneakers membership got me back into a workout routine and eating healthier helped my body take in more good nutrients than bad. When your routine blood work from the doctor shows normal levels, without pharmaceuticals, it is a tremendous feeling of accomplishment.

I tell my clients of teenage years, and younger, I believe their success, with trance, will typically outshine those of an adult. That is because their imaginations have not yet been beaten down; for them, life is still full of possibilities. No matter when you decide to take that leap of faith and step out on your own, approach your endeavor with a childlike innocence that frees your mind and creativity. Forget the conditioned mindset you formed throughout your life, and as Joseph Campbell coined, "Follow your bliss." I hope my experience helps you to visualize what is still possible for you.

***

To contact Gary:
www.tranceformedhypnosis.com
www.healthypathinitiative.com
www.facebook.com/tranceformedhypnosis
www.facebook.com/healthypathinitiative
https://www.linkedin.com/in/gary-goodspeed-aa3805138/

Bennie McWilliams

If you were to ask most people that know Bennie to describe him in one word, most likely, the winning vote would be: PASSIONATE. When he believes in something, or someone, the world will know it. Bennie is as real as they come. He has an energy that uplifts and encourages those he comes in contact with. People are drawn to his presence.

Bennie is a self-made entrepreneur, who had the odds stacked against him. Although life had many struggles and challenges, he kept reaching for *the prize* and didn't give up. Bennie built his business over six, grueling years, and all of the blood, sweat and tears has finally started to pay off. He is a prime example of *determination!*

Bennie loves to help people find the courage and confidence to reach for the sky and soar to their highest potential. He has always had a passion for supporting and helping others make their dreams come true.

Today, Bennie is building a life coaching career helping other entrepreneurs with their own businesses. He often states, "There is no better knowledge than experience itself." Bennie passionately shares his own experiences in life and business to help others have a smoother and shorter ride to *the top!*

You Can Be Anything You Want, If You're Willing to Take Action

By Bennie McWilliams

How can I say this with such certainty? Because, I am living proof that if you want anything in life, and you believe in your own potential, it can become reality.

Strange Opportunities

One of the things I've come to realize, from this experience of starting my vaping business, is that we are all capable of accomplishing so much more than we will ever realize! Sometimes, following your gut and pulling the trigger is tough, but if you have a dream, and a little courage, you can accomplish anything you want bad enough!

My introduction to the vaping industry came when a friend of mine brought a guest on our annual camping trip, this guest pulled out an e-cig at the campfire. I had no idea what this thing was or what it did. When I asked him what he was doing, he replied, "I'm quitting smoking." After the conversation, I thought, there's no way I would ever do that! It looked like he was doing something illegal. Pretty much the same thing everybody else thought about e-cigs. No one had been educated on e-cigs, nor their purpose and effectiveness in breaking one of the most addictive habits known to man. Smoking!

He shared with me his story of trying and failing and trying again. It was literally my story, as well as, many of my friends. I got to know that guy over the years, and I was amazed as I watched him not only quit smoking but rebuild his life.

When I met him, he was living in his car with a tent in the trunk. He had lost everything and was starting over again. Within a few years of meeting him, he had become a very successful businessman with a vision and a dream. He went to work on a small idea and built a phenomenal business.

Anytime you meet a man or woman with a dream, and the courage to try to see that dream come true, you will see them move one obstacle after another to accomplish their goals.

Universal Struggles

When I started my vape business six years ago, I had a dream of making a difference and helping others make a change in their lives. That, to many, seemed impossible. I know personally the challenges associated with becoming a non-smoker. My wife and I had tried and failed more times than I care to confess. We had both been smokers for many years, and there were many times when we would try to quit. My method was to wake up in the middle of the night and eat snacks until I fell into a sugar-induced coma and crawled back to bed. My wife would get up in the morning and find wrappers all over the counter. I gained 20-30lbs each time I attempted to quit. We would also be so irritable that we could barely stand ourselves, let alone each other. If you've ever smoked and tried to quit, you know exactly what I'm talking about. When we tried our first e-cig we were amazed that there were no hard cravings, weight gain orirritability. The one thing that we knew we needed to do, was to work one-on-one with each customer, be encouraging, and let them know they are not alone and, that, for- once-and-for-all they could become a non-smoker, for life!

As humans, we all need the help and support of others, sometimes, in order to accomplish a hard task. Our method of one-on-one coaching allowed them to feel like they weren't alone; we were there for them throughout the process. If we could give that feeling to each and every customer that walked through our door, we believed, it would greatly affect our success rate in helping people accomplish their goals. They could be successful, and we would be by their side throughout the whole journey to help in every way possible.

Did I Mention That My Wife Wasn't 100% On Board Yet?

Now, I had to convince my wife this was a good opportunity for our family, but she was having a hard time letting go of the safety and security that comes with a corporate job. When I say the struggle to try something new and unproven is real, it was very real.

To make matters worse, we were trying to get back on our feet and had just bought an
$1800 car from a "buy here, pay here" lot, luckily, the lot owner was a friend of the family. Our credit was challenged to say the least, and we didn't have any money to put down, but we needed a car to get back and forth to work. He helped us out, and sold us a small, older Saturn with 180,000 miles. It took us forever to pay it off. Some months we had to go to his car lot and wash and clean the cars just to make the payment.

Maybe you've been in a tight spot like this before, if you haven't, let's just say it's a time of character building.

I often tell the story of the pizza cutter. There was a time when my wife was cutting our pizzas with a butter knife because we didn't have the money to spend on a pizza cutter.

One day, I was at a Dollar Store with a friend and I was super excited to see a pizza cutter for a dollar, so I bought it and I couldn't wait to take it home. I walked in the door saying, "Honey I've got you a gift," but when I pulled out the pizza cutter, she just looked at me kind of funny. So, obviously, I needed to explain. I said, "It's a pizza cutter, and now you never have to use a butter knife again!" She replied, "How did you buy that?" I told her I had bought it for a dollar with the change from getting groceries earlier. She was upset and said, "That was the dollar needed for gas to get you to work tomorrow."

So, let's just say, it was one of those days. That is a true story, that I'll never forget. I can never forget where I came from. Keeping times like that in the front of my mind helps to keep me humble and grounded.

Increasing Exposure

One of the things that helped my wife realize this incredible opportunity was the day we walked in to get our first e-cig at a local vape shop. There were customers taking numbers, just like we used to do at the DMV to get our auto tags before the internet. As we were waiting, we had several conversations with some of the other customers that were in line. There were people in that store from 100 miles away! That completely blew my mind! Who would travel so far for a product to help them stop smoking? People who were absolutely committed to making a change in their lives for the better!

There was this one couple, who hadn't smoked in 2 months, and credited vaping and this store, specifically, to their success. You could see the pride in their faces as they shared how this one action of quitting smoking had changed their lives. It was truly inspiring.

We talked the whole way home about everything we had seen. The number of customers waiting in line. We even figured the amount of money we had seen exchange hands. I could tell my wife was coming around. And, honestly, how rewarding it would be to help make a difference in the lives of others.

One of the key ingredients necessary to be truly successful, in any business, is the sense of contribution, adding value to others. It's hard to place a financial value to it, but if you could, it would be right at the top with products and services. The little drops of dopamine we get when we truly help another human being always seems to come at the right time, when we're feeling down or tired, or just exhausted. There's something about that personal connection that fuels us to continue to push past the pain associated with start-up business ownership.

One Caveat

That's when the lights came on, and she asked, "Are we really getting ready to do this?" She had one caveat. She said, "We need to first talk to our pastor before making a final decision." This, I wasn't expecting, and I wasn't sure he would understand the opportunity.

Let's face it, if you haven't smoked and struggled to quit, could you understand what people are willing to do or pay to be a non-smoker?

Regardless, she wanted to get his blessing before we did anything further. To his credit, he had been very successful in a couple of businesses in the past. I truly thought there was no way in hell that this was ever going to happen.

Anyway, we set up a meeting and went to talk to the pastor. He drilled me for a couple of hours with questions, which I had all the answers for. When he finished, his advice was, "Well, you'll never know unless you pull the trigger, but be sure to stay true to your integrity and your character and you'll be fine." And then, he said jokingly, "How do I get in?" We did make him a consulting board member, and he is with us to this day.

The Difference Needed

In order to accomplish our objective, and remove the stereo type portrayed by most vape shops, everything needed to be different, both the atmosphere and the vibe. It was important that when our clients walked into our shop, that it was different, that they didn't feel like they had just walked into a typical "head shop". I wanted a classy, comforting atmosphere where we could, honestly, educate and support at the same time. We wanted to tie the community together by hosting an "open mic" night to showcase local artists. Mentally, I knew we needed to be part of our community to create a tribe, so that people would feel at ease and relaxed. Only then, could we earn their trust, and we could begin the process of educating people about the truth of vaping, instead of the scare tactics they were hearing in the media.

Political Oversight

One area, that I didn't realize how deeply I would need to be involved, was the political arena. A couple weeks after we opened our doors, I was informed that our state legislature was trying to pass legislation that would shut down our industry and close the doors to my business. I can't tell you the psychological havoc this news played on me. In an instant, I saw our new business possibly closing and my dream of entrepreneurialism was in danger. Interestingly, how quickly these thoughts found their way into my head.

If given the opportunity, I knew I could make a difference, and help others regain their health, but I needed to stay in business to accomplish this task. I thought, "There is no way I can sit back and just let this happen." Everything I owned, and some I borrowed, was tied up in this business. I could not fail.

Suit Up

If the politicians are going to involve themselves in our industry, so shall I! As the saying goes, "If it's worth having, it's worth fighting for." Well, I was all in at that point. I had learned the alternative smoking industry, I had been successful in the corporate community, now I was determined learn to navigate the political environment.

So, I became totally immersed in advocating for our industry. This ended up being both on the state and federal level. I invited all of our local legislators to come to our store so that I could give them a tour of our shop and educate them on the truths about vaping, what we do, how we do it, and share our mission to help everyone become a little healthier.

My first objective was to join our three local chambers of commerce and attended all meetings, about six or more a month. It was very intimidating to walk into a Friday morning chamber meeting with 145+ people knowing most were judging me because of the things they had heard about my industry.

At this time, the popular belief consisted of speculations about the unknown effects of vaping. Also, being reported to the public, was that the e-liquid we used, in our vaping material, was made from anti-freeze. They had even falsely reported vaping would give you pneumonia. Customers would come into our store asking our staff about the use of formaldehyde and embalming fluid in our products. All of this was, absolutely, 100% false! They didn't have a clue as to how these chemicals were related to vaping; but, it made good newspaper copy.

There have been multiple research studies, backed by bias organizations, that would stand to lose a lot of money if this industry was successful. This misinformation has since been dis-proven by the Royal College of Physicians stating that, "Vaping is at least 95% less harmful than smoking."

Most of them left with a different perception of what vaping is all about, and the great things that it can do for so many people.

Together, with our local chamber, we went to Washington DC to meet with our representatives. Two full days of walking Capitol Hill with back-to-back meetings. What an experience! They totally had our backs throughout this journey.

Testing Your Steel

There were many times when I wondered, is this really worth it? I felt very discouraged at times. It would have been so much easier not to go to those meetings and convince myself that it wasn't going to do any good. Especially after working at the store open-to- close, seven days a week for the first year and a half. Right when I was about to give in something happened that gave me hope.

The most important thing I want you to extract from this chapter is to always keep your integrity and character in check, and don't ever forget why you set out on your journey.

Understand there will be a price that needs to be paid to reach your goal. So, the question becomes, "Are you willing to do the hard work necessary to accomplish it?" Don't ever let anyone or anything pull you down. It's bad enough that you pull yourself down. You must stay true to your heart and your gut. So always rely on yourself. However, if you have doubts, turn to the people in your life that are there for you and will guide you and give you the right type of advice.

By the way, I had just used the kids' vacation savings to help open my first store, in hopes of making a difference in this industry, and creating a better future for my family. A few years prior, we had just begun rebuilding our lives after losing everything. Funds for this adventure were very tight. A 401K, savings account, and kids vacation fund were all we had to get started. We took everything we had and put it towards a chance at a dream. We were determined to make this work! And work we did!

The Price

There were so many sacrifices along the way, missed family get togethers, holidays, kids' birthdays, time with friends, sleep and the list goes on and on. We worked open-to- close, 7 days a week for the first year and a half, and my wife kept her other job during this time as well, all just to pay the bills at home. I can remember the first day we were able to take a day off and not go into the shop. We both sat at home that morning not knowing what to do with ourselves. It was a very strange feeling.

Our passion for the business was the only thing that kept us going. I knew from all of our customers' testimonies that we were making a difference in so many lives. Vaping was working for so many people.

Numerous times after working with a customer and getting them set up, they would come back and tell us of their experience and they would be in tears, in disbelief, and with so much hope because they hadn't had a cigarette for a week or for a month. Some of these people had smoked 50+ years and nothing had worked for them until now. These were overwhelming experiences for us and that kept us going along with our faith. We weren't giving up! Seeing our customers wanting something so bad, and my wife and I being willing to fight through the challenges is how we came up with our slogan: *"Education is our goal. Your Success is our passion, and quitting is just the Beginning"*.

We are now in the process of building our second, great business helping new business owners navigate the challenges associated with building and scaling their companies.

We've learned a lot in the last six years, everything from attracting and retaining the best talent, to increasing revenues and creating new income vehicles. Our goal is to help you define and implement the right strategies to grow and create a lasting change in your industry.

Things I've Learned Along the Way:

- Choose an industry you're passionate about and, then, dominate that industry!

- Know your why! Why are you willing to push yourself this hard?

- Clearly define what success looks like for you. How will you know when you reach it?

- I came to realize that to really become successful I needed to become and

  remain teachable. So, I read every business book I can get my hands on. I watch every YouTube video on business and listen to podcasts constantly. There cannot be enough said about self-education, and with the advent of social media, we are literally one click away from the greatest minds in business today; I became a professional "clicker"!

- Be aware of who you share your visions and dreams with. Surprisingly, not all are supportive. I've noticed, as I'm sure you have as well at times, the ones you think you can count on, you can't. I'm not sure why this is. Maybe our attempt to become more makes them uncomfortable.

- The struggle is real, but when you pass through the struggle you learn, adjust and move forward. When things got hard and I felt like giving up I put on that suit again and kept on fighting. There is no room for failure especially when you believe so deeply in what you're doing.

- If you take nothing else from this, make sure you take some time for yourself, find a quiet place, and simply breathe.

- Listen to those you respect, gain as much knowledge as possible, and give back to anyone who asks for your help.

- There are going to be entrepreneurs with that same look in their eyes that will reach out to you for advice and guidance.

- Never look back, unless it is to see how far you've come.

- There are so many more doors that are going to open up for you, be prepared to receive them.

- Don't let yourself get so in-over-your-head that you're stressed out and you're not having fun anymore. You're in this to win it. So, have fun doing it!

- Reward yourself along the way. Allow yourself to have the fun, that is what you deserve for all of the hard work and sacrifices.

***

Contact To contact Bennie:

https://www.facebook.com/bennie.w.mcwilliams

bennie@ecigloungemn.com

http://www.linkedin.com/in/benniemcwilliams

https://www.instagram.com/vapeninjamcw/

763-957-2019

JaNelle Garner

JaNelle is CEO and Founder Bliss Entertainment. She holds an Associates Degree in business management and is a communication specialist. JaNelle established Bliss Entertainment Studios Inc. in 2008 after working in service industry for 25

years. JaNelle has managed several businesses, and acquired invaluable experience with knowledge, skills and creativity that will help make Bliss Entertainment Studios Inc. successful in a relatively short time. JaNelle is the visionary and one of the creators for BLISS products, which she dedicated the last 20+ years.

Entrepreneurship is the Ultimate Incredible Journey

By JaNelle Garner

The world of an entrepreneur is not only an incredible journey it is a lifestyle of building amazing skill sets. In the last several years as an entrepreneur, the most important thing that I have learned is that you must be obsessed with your passion to survive the journey. My journey as an Entrepreneur started over 25 years ago and has been one of the most life-changing and educational experiences I have ever had. All of us are born with the talents and instincts to be entrepreneurs. However, not everyone understands how to achieve the goals to become a successful entrepreneur. A lot of people believe that it is too hard and thus don't pursue their dreams.

In this chapter I will share what I have learned and hope that it will guide you to a successful journey and put you on a path to understanding how to become a more effective you. When I started my journey, I knew it was going to be about changing education.

However, I had no idea how I was going to accomplish this mission. I knew nothing about business, including starting one, so I looked into taking some college courses for business. I decided to enroll at a local University in my home town. I signed up for several different business courses, hoping that I would learn how to open and operate a business. Even though I learned some valuable information, the courses I enrolled in did not help me with what I really wanted to know. I realized I had to find different outlets to learn the tools I needed to not only open a business but be successful at it. I decided to reach out and find different outlets that were teaching the tools needed to be successful in running a business.

I discovered many different resources, making it confusing as to where to begin. For the next several years I attended many different seminars that taught different skills and had resources for different things you needed to know and understand in order to build a strong business. These are some of the tools I learned that really helped me understand business:

* Becoming a powerful networker quickly builds strong business relationships and gets the contacts you need to keep moving your business forward.

* Becoming a successful entrepreneur is a full-time business; not a job but your passion.

* Find the right experts in the different fields needed to accelerate your business.

* Study how to develop the different departments your company needs to succeed; in other words, how to become "chief cook and bottle washer". You must understand each aspect of your business in order to run it properly.

* Research and development are crucial. You need to know what your market is, who your consumers are and if there is a need for the product or service you are selling.

These are just a few of the skills I discovered as I ventured into the entrepreneurial world. The more outlets I found, the more I learned about how to build my business. I also learned that the process is long. I spent many hours developing different techniques to move myself up to different knowledge levels in business.

Sometimes things moved fast, raising my excitement and passion. Other times nothing happened at all, which proved to be most discouraging. But I was not about to give up. I had a mission to accomplish and I knew that the more knowledge I learned, the more effective I became in getting things done. I was on a journey to change education and develop a new learning system, yet I had no idea how I was going to accomplish such a task. In fact, most of the experts I spoke with did not know how to advise me on what I was trying to do mainly because it had never been done before in education.

A lot of the time I was on my own, searching out the experts in what I needed to learn to build this unique learning system. The knowledge I learned over the next several years was priceless and taught me so many different aspects of business that helped me advance into developing an amazing new learning system. My skills and knowledge increased as I learned more about the educational industry. Today I am an expert in the field of how education should be taught. Once I understood what I needed to learn and develop, I started to learn other skill sets to be able to develop this new system.

I started becoming an expert in many different fields such as educational curricula and procedures, licensing, manufacturing, marketing, writing business plans and projections, just to name a few. I was so excited to learn these different skills and I was always eager to share my knowledge with other entrepreneurs.

After the first several years in learning business, I knew I needed to find a good team to help me pursue this mission of changing education because I knew I couldn't do it alone. You know what they say: "Team Work Makes the Dream Work."

I eventually found my dream team and they have been with me, helping me for the last 25 plus years. Finding your dream team is very important because you need a strong team who has the same passions and ambitions as you do. I went through many different individuals before I found the right people. You probably will not find your dream team quickly. It will take time and understanding and a lot of patience and due diligence.

I could tell you so many different stories of things that we have gone through, the good and the bad but we would have to write a separate book about the journey because there has been so much that has happened in the last 25 plus years. What we have learned as a team is that it's all about the journey and the knowledge and the skills you learn that will help you build a successful business.

Throughout the years I have discovered a strong need to develop a better and more effective way to teach entrepreneurs how to build business faster and more efficiently. Even though there are many different outlets to learn business, there is no training place that I have found that has all the tools and outlets to help entrepreneurs take a business idea from the beginning all the way through to the marketplace.

When I started this venture, I was told it is about a 10-year process from concept to the marketplace. This is true and sometimes it takes even more time than that because obtaining funding for your project is not easy. But I always tell entrepreneurs that I meet to never give up on their dream and passions. You will win in the end if you just keep moving forward.

You will always run into problems, and issues that can set you back, but as you learn how to fix the problems, you become more powerful because your knowledge becomes greater and your vision becomes clearer. We learned that beta testing is very important and must be done to assure a good return in the marketplace. Your product development will improve as you beta test and you will be more successful in the marketplace because you know what the market is demanding.

Your skills become so polished that you learn how to develop better products and services because you understand the marketplace. The marketplace will welcome you and your products or services because of your vast knowledge of delivering what the marketplace is looking for and wanting.

Your sales will increase because the consumer really wants what you have developed. Your vision will also become clearer as you learn and understand how the market works.

We still have the first product prototypes we designed but they have changed in not only design but concept of how they work. Now we have what we call polished products that the consumer will be attracted to purchase.

Becoming an expert at networking is a big part of becoming a successful business owner. Learning how to network properly and effectively is an art form and once you conquer the networking process you will get the contacts you need to get you to the next stage in your business. There is an art to networking that you need to learn. Find other entrepreneurs who have a talent to network and have them teach you how they do it. Don't limit yourself. Talk to people that you interact with at business meetups. You never know where they will take you. Often, it's not who you know but who *they* know. You should always be talking to others about who you are and what you are doing.

Everywhere I go I network, and I have found that it has accelerated my progress in business. The more I network, the faster to the finish line.

There will be times when you will want to quit because it just seems too hard or you just believe it will never happen. NOT TRUE! Keep your vision in front of you, never let it get behind you. If you can see it, you can build it!

You only get better as you learn the process of business, and as your knowledge grows, so does your expertise. Because of what we have learned we have been able to advance our business and now we are positioned in such a way that when we enter the marketplace, we will have stronger success.

Again, you must be obsessed with your passion or you will never survive the journey. You have to believe that there is always another path that will take you down a more powerful road that will guarantee your success. I have learned that when one door closes it's because it's not the right path for you and you need to find the right door.

Over the last 25 years the knowledge and skills I have learned will not only help my team to become more successful, but it will help us to help other entrepreneurs become successful as well. We are now getting into our final stages of being able to showcase our business to the world and teach others to do the same thing. Giving back in business is important and it helps others to become successful in their endeavors.

As entrepreneurs, it is important that we teach each other how to play together and help each other grow. If we do this, we can change our communities and help the people grow into more effective individuals. Doing business in cooperation instead of competition will help everyone become a winner. There is room for everybody. Become a sponge for information and learning skill sets, because there is always something to learn that will help you and your business grow faster.

When I first agreed to do this chapter for Cracking the Rich Code, I was not sure why I was committing to such an amazing venture. Even though we have been in business for over 25 years, we only have one product on the market: a children's book. I thought to myself that we are just beginning to emerge into the marketplace and not yet successful. We have not cracked the rich code. Boy was I wrong.

Last night it hit me when I was finishing up this chapter: Cracking the Rich Code is not about having become rich or wealthy in business, it is about obtaining the knowledge and skills needed to become a successful entrepreneur, learning the art of becoming self-sufficient and learning to give back to others who need help. It's a way of life or a new lifestyle where you understand how to achieve goals that others don't know how to achieve. It sets you apart from others because you see life in a different light.

We have cracked the rich code! I am proud to say that we are now in a place in our business where we are positioning ourselves with big companies in the entertainment industry. All of the hard work and skills we have learned have brought us to this moment in time. The journey has been incredible, and our knowledge has grown to where we have now attracted the right people to get us to the marketplace and be successful.

We have designed and created one of the most amazing learning systems for education and entrepreneurs. Our products are loved by many people who have already had the opportunity to use them. The new companies we are working with love the merchandise we have developed, and they believe it will be very successful in the marketplace. We are currently working on getting a building to remodel to open our first showcase to help entrepreneurs grow faster, learn more effective business skills, develop new lifestyles and become self-sufficient.

This showcase will be highly interactive with 3D technologies, educational outlets that use whole brain learning with accredited classrooms for both students and adults. It will have an interactive restaurant starring the characters from our new storybook, "Lost Legend of the Tude Shifters" and the ensuing children's book series.

We will train entrepreneurs, starting at the age of 5 years old, in Professor Wallahoo's Fab Labs. The showcase will also have an entrepreneurial Convention Center where entrepreneurs can promote their businesses. It will feature retail outlets with great products and services, including a new space dome where there will be high-tech gaming, using new platforms that will blow your mind.

Inside the space dome you will also find a state-of-the-art STEM program where adults and children can learn the skills of science, math, technology, and electronics. These classrooms are also accredited. We have so much more of what we are doing but the showcase will help us get into the marketplace where we can help communities across the globe.

If you would like to learn more about who we are and what we are doing, we invite you to check us out at www.americandreamers4change.com (toateswackywonder@gmail.com).

Everything we do is to help educate children and adults and help them to become self-sufficient through our amazing interactive environments.

This has been the most incredible journey for me and my team and the valuable skills we have learned we can now teach to others. Our new journey is now beginning as we enter into an amazing world of education and entertainment. Our dreams and visions are becoming a reality because we kept our visions and passions in front of us, allowing them to blossom and grow. Let us help you do the same.

TOATES WACKY WONDER SHOWCASE

An experience that takes you out of Earth's Galaxy into the unknown. There you will travel through portals that take you on adventures of mystery, magic and fantasy…

A New Magical Experience for the entire Family.

WHAT HAPPENS INSIDE IS PURE MAGIC

A new type of community showcase designed to help people in their communities to learn effective business and entrepreneurism with a new EIT learning system developed for education. Plus, we have a place for shopping, entertainment, good food and just plain fun!

Inside Toates Wacky Wonder Emporium you will experience excitement that will last a lifetime… As you enter Toates Wacky Wonder Showcase you will be transported in a world of fun, magic, mystery, adventure and the most amazing learning experience on the planet!

IMAGINE

A place where you can go that will take you far away from the normal hustle and bustle of shopping. A relaxing place that gives you enjoyment when you shop, play and learn, it will take you into a world of fun characters that you can interact with, play with and more. **This is the Toates Wacky Wonder Showcase!**

We want to give our consumer an experience that will bring them back over and over again. With the economy the way it is today, all retailers are trying to re-invent themselves to get more consumers through their doors.

We believe we have a great solution to the problem, which is why we are building this great Showcase. The Showcase is designed to help people in their communities to reach their potential and build stronger communities. A place where people in the community can come together with their family and friends to help each other learn the tools to rebuild their communities in a unique environment. The Showcase provides programs with a new learning facility that will help the young and the old entrepreneur to grow and become more successful.

The consumer is looking for new things to excite them and engage them. We know we can do this inside the Showcase. Because of our technology and other technologies that are available today, we can change things over and over again to give new experiences inside the Showcase each time the consumer come in.

***

To contact Janelle:

toateswackywonder@gmail.com

Mariana Light

Mariana Light is a Divine Minister, an Intuitive Health, Nutrition, Life and Longevity Expert/Coach, Master Herbalist since 1996, Conscious Divine Centered Entrepreneur, Inventor, and Founder of an online business—Youth Eternal Supreme, through her ARP Tech Health. Through her unique gift of clairvoyance, she helps her clients develop their own gifts via education of the 1001 Universal Divine Laws of Life, which transform lives into a Divine way of living on all aspect of one's life, including the unlocking of your Life's Purpose and Mission, and most importantly above all, she offers guidance in how to fulfill one's own Divine Plan in this embodiment without fail. She is an innovative product researcher, developer, master formulator, and business consultant. Her unique innovations have blessed thousands across the world—for which she takes no credit for her outer self, but gives it all back to God and Its Christ Light. She is currently working on several health food recipe books and master self-help courses.

Introduction to Unlocking your Treasure House

By Mariana Light

The story of my life even as early as my childhood has led me to search for a deeper meaning in life and ask deeper questions like: who am I actually, beyond this body and name? Why am I here? What is the true purpose of my life beyond what society wants me to believe? What is the true purpose of all life and of all existence? Why is no one able to answer these simple questions, and why are there only theories and speculations? Why was mankind created in a first place? What is this life all about? Is there more to life than what is presented on the outer manifestation by others? The many hardships I have endured led me to ask: why is it that, besides the beauty of life, that there is still so much suffering, lack, and limitation in this world when we were all created equally and in the "Image and Likeness" of our all loving and infinitely abundant Creator God? Is suffering truly necessary, and why can't we all learn only from the points of beauty, happiness, and joy without lack and limitation? Is this possible?

I knew deep in my heart that human potential was so much greater than currently expressed on the outer, and that our Loving Creator would never make us to lack in any way—since no Supreme Intelligence, who has manifested such beauty and such intricate systems of existence and infinite ever expanding space, would ever create us to live in shortage of any good thing. I always held onto that faith, and hoped that more would be revealed to me to support my intuition and faith in God's supplying Light and the perfection of Its gift of life.

I never wanted to accept the hypnotic idea that suffering or problems were necessary; although I knew that somehow there must be a way to, not only transform all struggle into success—which to me is just a beginning level of life's mastery—but to block and prevent all limitations from manifesting and therefore becoming the true master of your destiny, a harmonious destination that you choose, while forbidding all limitations and mistakes. Is this possible? I always wondered. The outer world wanted me to believe that you need darkness in order to have Light, BUT that did not make sense to me. Why? Because Light truly does not need darkness to shine! If it did, then that would make the Eternal Source of all Life, which is the Divine Perfection of God dependent upon human limitations of discord. Since God's Light is the only true Masterful Presence of invincible supply and harmony, It does not depend on any limitations nor human opinions to create and sustain systems of worlds.

I knew that since the unconditional love of our Creator God is the force of all harmony—beyond the duality of good and bad as the Supreme Perfection of all creation—and since none here have created themselves, all life belongs to this supreme, Divine Love. THAT Love which has created us, which sustains our consciousness, and has given us the FREE WILL, also created the Universal Divine Laws of Life. So, if we live by them, we will be in balance in all aspects of our being, including our finances. Therefore, in our original divine blue print, if we abide by those laws of divine love, wisdom, and power, and do not deviate, then we will be in a resonant and harmonious state of being—rather than in discord. There must have been some formula or instructions for these Divine, Universal Laws of Life, right? If we had them all, we could apply them and prove they work, right? Yes, that is right, but not everybody is ready to purify all aspects of their world and let go of their human desires in order to live their Divine Plan, yet some day, some time, somewhere all will be compelled to seek the Light, for the love of living in Light alone, and join in service with Great Host of Light for the fulfillment of great, ever expanding Divine Plan.

Going a bit into my childhood, despite highs of amazing talent in dance, singing, art, and even performances I directed as a child who loved to help cheer up others with confidence and joy, I also had to stand, face, and conquer the deepest lows of my parent's abusive and broken marriage, and many other trials and tribulations that most people could not even imagine surviving. All were miraculously healed, as if I had group of Angels at my side. One of those Angels was Beloved Mother Mary—the mother of Jesus Christ—Beloved Jesus, and Beloved Saint Germain. I did not know much about them back then, until more experiences brought forth further Revelations and I was introduced to the Universal Divine Laws of Life. So, there are higher and higher octaves of existence and Beings of Light by whose love humanity is sustained and allowed to try again and again to expand into ones Higher Self. So much was shown to me that I finally understood that we too are meant to become higher versions of ourselves and evolve into our own eternal Divine Beings—which is and always was the original Divine Plan for us all upon the Earth. Yet humanity, by the misuse of one's power and the destructive use of one's free will, forgot their Source by focusing on outer manifestations rather than the inner and by falling into so many traps of evil dressed up as good. So many have failed and have had to re-embody and try again and again; yet there is a higher Divine Plan of not only living in heaven here and now, but of accomplishing next step of one's evolution into our eternal Divine Self that knows no lack nor limitation.

Being in uninterrupted harmony is the key to true Mastery of life, yet it takes the application and embodying the Divine Laws of Life to out picture that here and now. What does it matter if one has abundance of money, yet lacks in invincible health, harmonious relationships, or that liberating feeling of only pouring out love and blessings to all life? Plus, most important above all, what does it all matter if one has not connected to Its Higher Self and ones Source of Life where all answers are on how to fulfill ones Divine Plan according to the requirements of the Supreme Love of THAT Divine Law, rather than one's own human concepts?

Therefore, if one choses to live consciously and blesses all life with their feelings, thoughts, words, and deeds—regardless if the individual deserves it or not—and learn to conquer the feeling of resistance, one will make it a habit to call forth God's healing Light into every person, place, condition and thing. If this can be accomplished without judgment or opinion, then that same harmonious energy will be returned to you, only amplified. It will come back and bless you with EVERY GOOD THING, including money. You will become a blessing to all you contact. This may be easy if someone is kind to you, but it may take more mastery in knowledge and application of the Divine Laws, especially when you are facing injustice, yet there is your greatest opportunity.

When you call forth Light—the only Master, the Highest Intelligence—Its force moves into action and knows exactly what needs to be done. If there is something required of you, you will receive an idea about what is the right thing to do. You are the caller, and God's Light is the doer. Not having feelings of resistance does not mean accepting something that is not right; it means you must watch and master your own feelings, so you do not fall into traps of judgment, and therefore attract that same thing in different format to yourself. It also does not mean allowing someone to continue their discord. Remember, you are never without God's Light and help. It is only a thought, a feeling, away. In fact, God's Light is closer to you than your own hands and feet; it is the life that sustains you.

There are over 1001 Universal Divine Laws of Life, and their application will help you to evolve into your true treasure house— which includes, but is beyond, riches. I am here to help point you to master yourself and your world. I am not a guru, but I will point the way to your only and true Teacher, your Individualized Presence of God and Its Laws—whether you know it or not, whether you believe it or not. When you learn to depend solely upon it, you will have the keys to the all supplying treasure house. To reach It, is to know how to purify the veils in between.

So, NO! We do not have to learn from crisis, and YES we can be helped to prevent and dissolve all of our negative past Karma and destructive etheric records. It all must be dealt with if one is to have their PATHWAY CLEARED OF ALL OBSTACLES—not only to your financial freedom, but so far beyond. Financial freedom is important, but if you do not work on your Ascension and escaping the wheel of birth and rebirth all over again, you will not have the full satisfaction becoming the master over all energy in your world here and now, in a harmonious way while infinitely evolving into a greater being in an infinite creation.

So much was revealed to me; and there is a divine way to open your treasure house in every aspect of your being. I was shown exactly where to find this and have been sharing it with all of my clients who are proving this to themselves. You can do it, too. If you are ready to fly above human struggles and limitations, and free yourself from the wheel of birth and rebirth, you must become of service to life for the return of Heaven on Earth, rather than just chasing money and material gain. That alone will never bring you everlasting happiness.

Although important, financial success is one of the lesser accomplishments in the true scheme of life. Once one learns to live according to the Divine Laws of Life, one will be fully rounded in happiness, health, joy, and financial freedom. If money is accumulated by harming others, one will never have the ability to truly enjoy it and will lack in so many other aspects of life. Only by living in accord, in harmony with the Universal Divine Laws of Life, can one become truly Divine, conquer all lower human tendencies, and finally fulfill one's original Divine Plan.

Therefore, you must become a master of your own world. You are not here to master others, but to master the energy of your own life in a constructive way that is harmonious to all life. Material wealth is only energy; if you master energy, you will have plenty. Then, if you do not fail to use it for that which is only harmonious to all life, you will be able to enjoy it and become a magnet that will draw to yourself more and more harmonious experiences and blessings. This is why a Conscious Entrepreneur of today must create and offer only that which is truly harmonious. Your words, feelings, deeds, and all you allow into your consciousness is the key to your success.

Many people know something of the Law of Attraction, yet do not know much about the Law of Repelling and Forbidding, and other important Laws that must accompany it. There is nothing harmonious and good that does not already belong to you. Once you learn how to no longer participate in the misconceptions and traps of this world, you will be free to start your Ascension of consciousness, body, mind, and being into your Divine Self, and at the close of this embodiment you will earn your next existence above human, not having to return back and try all over again.

If you look at all outer expressions of life from the perspective of energy, frequency, and vibration, then apply the Divine Laws of Life every day, you will understand that all physical things, all circumstances, all substance, places, and conditions are energy returning back to us from our own thoughts, words, deeds, and feelings in accumulation from this and all past embodiments. All energy can be purified and transmuted into the victories of Light, and all of our past mistakes can be purified and cleansed, so that you no longer experience obstacles and limitations. You, I, and everyone else, are all here in order to master OUR own worlds. How it can be accomplished is more important than the food you eat. To me, being able to guide you is a privilege and honor, and I have proven this method to myself. All must master the lower human tendencies and become the expression of that "image and likeness of God" to which we were all created to express. We can call God's healing Light into life and into all individuals, and we can give people temporary help, but we cannot be a crutch because all must learn to reach up to their own individualized Presence of God—your Source of all life, all Intelligence, all happiness, all supply, and all riches of every good thing you can ever require and desire. In the fullness of that Presence is all you could ever need and beyond.

As my friend, Beloved Jesus the Christ says, "Ye are your Brother's and Sister's Keepers", yet most people do not understand we are all brothers and sisters from One Creator God, regardless of human opinions and we are to call God's Light into our brothers and sisters lives, not only when we see them go array, but also when things are going well for the invincible expansion and protection of all good and for those who are constructive in this world. None of us are an Island on its own; that means we need to bless everyone with our feelings, thoughts, words, and deeds of Divine Love and Light. What happens when someone is bound in darkness and the all-powerful God's Light appears? What happens in a room full of darkness when the light switch goes on? If one is indifferent to loving all life, one cannot and will not have the lasting riches and supply of <u>every good thing</u>! There will be some lack and limitation. Love and Light does not mean weakness. Remember, Light means Power over all darkness! Energy Acts! It is not a respecter of persons, titles, or human opinions. It will go out from a sender in a circle, collect more of its own similar expressions, and return it back to the sender.

Remember, you are always dealing with the energy of God's pure Light, and if you misuse that energy to hurt someone else, or to judge, or to have feelings of condemnation, frustration and irritation, then you will have to experience that yourself until you learn how to master all those lower expressions of limitation. If you instead choose to call forth God's Power of Light into all persons, places, and things then that Light will go forth and do what is necessary.

People sometimes ask me what about products and businesses that have produced harmful elements, yet there is a seeming abundance from that. According to the Divine Beings of Light, that cycle is closing. In the incoming Golden Age, only that which is harmonious to all life will be able to prosper in any way and create true and ever-expanding abundance. They also speak of times when mankind will be able to return to their Divine Origins, and that many will start using their full brain potential—versus now which is below 10%, and that many advanced souls will be able to precipitate again from the Universal substance, therefore not needing a commercial way of exchange.

Most people do not know how important it is to purify the energy from all past embodiments. Even if you are financially set, you will still have many other aspects of your being and world to clear, develop, purify and expand your consciousness. You need to know how to accomplish this and keep expanding unto your higher and higher potential.

I say this because, in true reality, there is only <u>infinitely expanding potential.</u> There is no fullest potential because life is ever expanding and infinite. And, since you are life, your being is meant to expand indefinitely into greater and greater. However, if these past and present life patterns are not cleansed and kept purified, one may find oneself with too many obstacles in fulfilling one's constructive goals, or one may not feel the full satisfaction of life that is only found in living by the Divine Laws of Life. If you do not know how to clear the way with the use of Light Rays, and if you do not know anything about your Divine Plan or how to fulfill it, one will only be experimenting with one spoke of a wheel and will feel emptiness on some level.

Are you ready to learn about your Divine Potential that will make financial freedom a byproduct of FAR GREATER RICHES directly from your source's treasure house, plus help this world become Heaven on Earth for all humanity?

***

To Contact: Mariana

www.YouthEternalSupreme.com

mariana@youtheternalsupreme.com

Future Courses: www.IamTheMastery.com

Danny Kerridge

Hi, Danny Kerridge here. I entered the Plastic Injection Moulding profession as an operator in the early eighties and ended up a lecturer for TAFESA in 2015. I entered a factory career as a stop-gap whilst looking for my chosen career. Funny how life points you in a certain direction.

Whilst learning my trade, I noticed that there was plenty of technical information around, in books at the time, now over the internet. Initially, one had to learn from somebody else—picking up on terminologies and the way they do things or get around certain issues. Even today, there is little for the newbie in this industry. You need to reach a certain level before things make total sense—just doing things verbatim from someone showing you the ropes. This, I always thought, opened one up to learning bad habits and traits; so, these thoughts led me towards writing a Meat-and-Potatoes (elementary) look into why and how things are done in the Plastic Injection Moulding arena. With much feedback, I have now completed an in-depth, ready reference guide with links to terminologies, tricks and fixes suitable for the newbie and the seasoned technician.

Life's Journey

By Danny Kerridge

Isn't it amazing how the universe and actions/reactions work? When you come right down to it, the universe works in really amazing ways. How we find our way in life, is it fate, is it destiny or just a series of decisions?

Like many other people on this planet, I left school not knowing what I wanted to do, achieve or aspire to. As it ended up, I joined the Royal Navy for around four years. This instilled in me the training and dedication I would need to continue my life. Little did I know at the time, l was not happy with the course I was taking. Yes, all was professional and I learnt a trade as well as how to follow orders, etc. But again, like so many others, this just didn't fit with what I wanted out of life.

So, I left the services. My two brothers were bus drivers; so I joined them, driving buses for the government in my local city. I was content at this, meeting the public, getting Mary or Joe to their destinations on time. It fulfilled my love of driving. But, after nine years, I started getting concerned that I wanted a career, you know, one of those things you go to every day and end up showing others the ropes—wherein satisfaction, contentment, money, assets and all life has to offer stems from. In reality, I got married while I worked driving buses and wanted a more (shall we say) professional attitude toward life to support my family. I have nothing against bus drivers; in fact, I enjoyed my years on the buses. I just wanted more out of life. So, I resigned from driving and took a position as an operator in plastics, sitting on a machine sorting defective parts as a stop-gap to finding what was in my heart. It was here that l started to notice what the technicians were doing to fix my machine when it went wrong. Now, I had a mechanical background—my father owned his own auto repair garage—so I grew up around mechanical things, which made my ears prick up.

When the machine I was on went awry, whilst the technician was at lunch, I made the adjustments necessary. Of course, I told the technician when he came back. Well, after a while I started to get noticed by management in fixing the machines when no-one was available. They thanked me for taking the initiative and keeping the technicians informed. Truth is, at that time I didn't always make the right adjustments, but by informing the technicians I not only kept it (let's say) professional, I got the opportunity to continue learning when the technician pointed out where I may have gone wrong. This inspired me to read the setup sheets and look even deeper into the workings of Plastic Injection Moulding and its processes. Management could see some potential in me and asked if I was prepared to learn and take on material handling—the first step up the ladder, which consisted of working out when and which machine needed more material, different material or whether that material needed drying before being put into the machine. Needless to say, my ears pricked up even more.

I started my journey into something that kept me thinking, *why did that machine act that way? Why did that material react that way to the mouldings?* I was hooked. To this point, I hadn't felt good about myself or where I was heading. Sure I left school, joined the Navy, and I got all the professional schooling the Navy is known for— ranks, obeying orders, doing the right thing by fellow servicemen etc—but something had been missing until now.

So… I was set up from that point to tackle life head-on. The buses, it seemed, were the stop-gap for me finding my passion. I went from strength to strength in the Plastic Injection Moulding industry and soon rose up the ranks because of my professionalism and expertise on finding the right course of action. This all culminated in me lecturing at TAFESA (Technical and Further Education in South Australia). The climb wasn't easy, I had to fully understand what I was doing. Over the years I witnessed some serious injury, and on one occasion a death, from not using the correct procedures.

I loved getting to know my (felt right) trade, and I insisted on passing this knowledge onto others. Itchy feet saw me transfer to a different company a few times over the years, and there was always the go-to technician who got the job done and had all the fixes, but wouldn't pass on his secrets. This went against my grain. Why not tell everyone how you fix these issues and raise everyone's bar or level of knowledge? You know, together we rise, individually we fall. This fell on deaf ears, so I started informing everyone I could on how I fixed a particular issue. I went into depth on why this worked to whomever asked or wanted to know. This, of course, put me in the bad books with the so called "mister fixit" technicians. But you know, I started to discover that these technicians that had all the answers were typically long-term employees who had seen all the fixes over the years and knew what worked and what didn't work. But my industry upbringing at that stage had insisted that I understand what worked and why it worked. So, I asked these technicians why a particular fix that they put in place worked. You know (and this still amazes me), a lot of the time they couldn't answer the question, other than to say, "It always works for me."

So, as time went by, the fixes I put in place started to get recognized. And when asked, I informed everyone exactly why it worked (to the best of my understanding) and soon enough, these technicians warmed up to me on why a particular fix worked. Now, understand I didn't have all the answers, but what I did have was getting to the bottom of why a particular fix actually worked. Over time, this snowballed my understanding in the Plastic Injection Moulding field.

It was inevitable that eventually I would end up lecturing on why things worked and educating others in this field. The universe had not only led me to a career that I enjoyed, but graded a path to further that career.

Of course, I had to make the decisions that finally led me to this point. Eventually, because of the start I had in this industry—what with the fix-all technicians keeping things to themselves—there wasn't much information in books or on the internet that showed newbies in the industry what they should be doing. There has always been highly technical stuff around, but very little on steering the complete newbie on terminologies and what they should be doing in very basic form. Even now, there is very little basic information in this Plastic Injection Moulding field. This prompted me to write a book entitled 'Meat and Potatoes of Plastic Injection Moulding: Introduction to Basic Elements and Why We Use Them.' That is quite a mouthful, I know, but it is exactly what I wanted to publish—elementary terminologies and skills that the complete newbie needed in order to progress in the industry.

Well, after feedback from this book, even experienced technicians contacted me and asked that another book be produced. So, I wrote the 'Meat and Potatoes of Plastic Injection Moulding: Troubleshooting.' This offered insights into helping the more seasoned in Plastic Injection Moulding. Again, after feedback, I have written yet another book which outlines step-by-step procedures to fix particular issues. It describes in more depth and in very basic language why a particular order is most efficient and why it works. More than this, the book explains terminologies; all is linked within the book.

I was brought up in England and the term 'Meat and Potatoes' means an elementary look or to get to the basics, root essence of the meaning. Hence, my book title. I believe this fixes a shortfall in the industry. There are a lot of technical books and information around, but it is not until you have been in the industry a number of years that you fully understand what is being said or what you are reading. And can relate to what is happening in the mould.

My Journey broken down

I started life as an adult willing to try anything, like so many others in the world. I earned to stick with a career until I retire, but it didn't feel right initially. It was only when I made the decision to change that things started working out for me. Don't get me wrong, these were not easy decisions to make, but I was convinced I had to try something else. More than that, I knew I had the conviction to carry that decision through to its completion (thanks to the Royal Naval training).

The buses felt right, but I wanted more for my family. I also knew I could fall back on driving if my decision was the wrong one. In life you can't fear making a decision; you can always change that decision, but if you don't try, then you will never know, right? I heard someone say once, 'don't waste your life wondering what if.' And that is so right! Give it a go and never wonder.

You must also recognize when you have arrived. I knew shortly after starting as a machine operator that this captured my interest. You need to know and accept when that point hits home to you. What I am trying to say is this: I changed from the Navy to buses, completely different fields. From there, I became a factory worker, again completely different fields. Take, for example, if you change from one factory job to another factory job; unless you're rising up the ladder or receiving a promotion, then you are not aligning with the universe and what it wants to show you.

I have managed to fulfill a need in the Plastic Injection Moulding industry that I noticed was missing. I have made it available around the world. My work fills a need for the newbie as well as the seasoned veterans in the industry. This has been my contribution to the industry. It has also helped open up the secret fixes, previously hidden.

Now more than ever, juniors have a 'go to' reference book to relate to and try out specific fixes that previously had been hidden. This action is helping to grow the industry as a whole. Take for example a long-term technician who always fixes a particular job when it goes wrong. He is on day-shift, it is now 4 in the afternoon, and no-one else knows how to fix the issue. So, the machine gets turned off until the technician arrives the following morning and puts his fix into action. The company has lost nearly two shifts of production and still no-one else knows how to remedy this if it happens again. (Don't laugh, I have seen this happen over the years—quite a few times). Now, the newbie can reference a book and not only put a fix in place, but get a complete understanding on why this fix should work. If it doesn't work, there is a step 2, then 3 etc. until the right fix is in place. With complete instructions on what is happening, when and why you put this fix in place is the difference between success and time lost.

It is not my intent to have every reader question their own journey. This is my life's journey and how it eventuated. My website, if you are in the Plastic Injection Moulding arena, is (yes you guessed it):

https://www.injection mouldingtips.com.

I hope your journey is as fruitful as mine has been, but more than that, I hope the satisfaction you get from your knowledge and expertise in whatever field you are in makes you smile….smile in a way that you know you have made it.

Twitter: https://twitter.com/yesdan

Facebook: https://www.facebook.com/danny.kerridge

LinkedIn: http://www.linkedin.com/in/dannykerridge

email: dankerr4u@gmail.com

website: https://www.injectionmouldingtips.com

Become a coauthor in the next Cracking the Rich Code book
http://www.beacoauthor.com/Danny

Ed Keener

Ed Keener (INTJ) is an entrepreneur specializing in web development for fellow entrepreneurs. He has an appreciation for network marketers and enjoys helping bring their vision to life. His family resides in Seattle (SeaTac) Washington where they work, attend church and school. Having grown up in an Air Force family constantly on the move, Ed is accustomed to changes that life brings. He has worked in serval technology fields starting with avionic electronics while serving in the Alaska Air National Guard. Through the years he's gained experience in telecommunications, electronic banking, computer networking, and real estate. With an appreciation for creativity and technology, web design and development are a natural fit for his personality.

Ed and his family enjoy traveling abroad, going to theme parks, and RV camping in the great Pacific Northwest. His hobbies include gardening, woodworking, and watching The Flash and Eureka episodes with his teen daughter. He has varying interests which include innovative technologies, physics, astronomy, and creating the perfect beef stew recipe.

Ed's services include freelance web design, website hosting, and technical consultation. He is in the development phase of creating his own network, AffiliateAlliance.ws, which will provide website hosting, education, and incorporate an affiliate program for online entrepreneurs.

Lead, Follow or Get Out of The Way

By Ed Keener

That was the motto that greeted me to my Basic Military Training Squadron, the 3707th, in October of 1988. I was 19 years old at the time riding in a blue bus along with a bunch of other fresh recruits. Most of them had enlisted in the Air Force while I chose to enlist in the Alaska Air National Guard. Even so, the same training was required. Lead, follow or get out of the way. I pondered upon those words while waiting to disembark the bus. Some people seemed naturally endowed with leadership qualities while others work overtime to develop leadership know-how; but what is it to be a great leader? What's the "right stuff"? Some would cite a take-charge attitude, or a magnetic, charismatic personality, or one that exudes an aura of authority commanding respect of those around them. While these are certainly valuable assets for leadership, I submit that what makes a *great* leader is the heart of a servant.

I am a Christian. I mention this because to understand a little about who I am you must first know Whose I am. My Christian faith is an integral and inseparable part of me that influences my philosophy, thought process, and decision making.

In the scripture, there is a lesson of leadership like no other and can be found in the book of John chapter 13. You do not have to share in my Christian faith to glean the truth from this telling. It recounts the story of Jesus and His disciples had gathered in a room and lingering after sharing a meal. Jesus quietly gets up and prepares a basin of water and gets a towel. One by one He kneels at His followers' feet unbuckles their sandals and proceeds to wash their feet. Is there a humbler station than this? The King of Kings, Lord of Lords, the Christ, Son of the Living God, the One who spoke the universe into existence is kneeling before those that call Him master and washing their feet. Imagine for a moment this historic scene. His followers were rather taken back by this action, never conceiving this act as possible. And yet Jesus persisted in this way to serve those that followed Him.

Now as a young man of 19 I was cognitively aware of this principle. However deeper appreciation and real-world application came along with age. In business, it's natural for us to look out for number one. But one major aspect of network marketing businesses appealed to me. In order have great success in network marketing you must put the interest of others before your own. By profession, I am a freelance web developer. So, I use my skills and talents to augment the online tools of my downline. This might mean creating unique lead capture pages, email forms, or page rotators. Whatever is needed by the team to elevate them. Their success then becomes my success because I have chosen to serve their needs. Chances are that your abilities lie elsewhere but many skills are easily transferable to growing a network. Are you bilingual? Do you excel in public speaking? Maybe you have great organization skills or are artistic. Whatever the ability, seek to apply it to serve those that follow you into the business. Maybe you're just getting started and do not have a downline. I suggest communicating with your upline and other members of the team and inquire about what their needs are. I promise you; your efforts will not return void. You will be a blessing to others and in turn, be blessed.

Focus at What You're Aiming At

As a teenager, my sister and I would often spend weeks at a time during the long days of summer. time visiting my grandparents in Nikiski, Alaska during the long daylit summer months. A nearby property owner had kept huskies but in a very irresponsible fashion. The dogs roamed freely and bred until they numbered greater than a hundred. Half domesticated, half-wild, these dogs would pack up and invade bordering properties and create concern for safety. It got to the point that my grandpa had to use his .22 rifle to either scare them away or, if they did the mistake of returning, put them down. He loathed having to kill dogs but did not see any other alternative. One sunny afternoon, three dogs appeared at the end of the gravel drive. My grandpa brought out his .22 but I pleaded with him to allow me to scare them away. It did not take much convincing on my part. I grabbed a rock that fit neatly in the palm of my hand. The middle dog, the leader, was watching me and we locked eyes. The three of them just stood there roughly 20 yards away from us, observing. Keeping my eyes dead on the lead dog I reached out and lobbed that rock with a high arc into the air. With the dog and I gazing at one another, time seemed to be suspended as I waited for the rock to reach its intended target. Suddenly my grandpa and I heard a loud crack while the lead dog simultaneously let out a loud yelp and collapsed on all fours. The rock had found its target square on the top of the dog's head. With incredulous haste, the lead dog then leaped up and all three vanished, never to be seen again. My grandfather and I had trouble catching our breath with all the laughter of having witnessed this spectacle. After gaining his composure, my grandpa exclaimed: "You should have let me shoot the dog, it would have hurt less!" Maybe so, but they all got to live a little longer and perhaps warned their friends to stay away from that place.

If you desire to hit your mark, you must remain focused upon it. There is a lot of noise in our modern world vying for our attention. There are various methods one may employee (network marketing, affiliate marketing, direct sales, product creation, and so on) by which money can be made. There are many fine companies one can choose to align themselves with. Allowing ourselves to be sidetracked by the latest shiny object will only serve in separating our money from our pockets and distract us from the prime target. Pick a heading and stay true to the course. Exercise patients and work the system that's laid out before you. After that operation takes root and begins to grow more on its own accord, then lift your head and allow yourself to seek out other opportunities. Once you have found the next venture, rinse and repeat. This is how to build multiple streams of income. It begins with focus.

Putting Your Best (Digital) Self Forward

During my short stint as a real estate agent, my mentor taught me something of importance that I'll never forget. I had asked him why he changed real-estate firms and if he was concerned over the impact it would have on his clientele base. He explained that the new firm offered more favorable terms than his previous one had. Then to address part two of my inquire he replied "People do business with people. They do not care about which real-estate company you're with."

While there are varying aspects of what makes one online marketer more successful than their fellow marketers, I'll be focusing upon one vital aspect. Something I had observed early on my exploration of network marketing was that the highly successful marketers had an online presence all their own. They do not rely upon a company replicated websites but create their own. Lead capture, newsletter, you name it, it's their own. Why? Because people do business with people. Promote yourself first and then present your business opportunity. Whatever the affiliate program or network marketing company you're aligned with matters less. Most likely there are plenty of other reps in the same network as you are. Be uniquely you and give people a reason why they should join you, not your network company. What carries great importance is making a personal connection with people in your team. Here I'll be sharing some practical and actionable insights on how you can present your best digital self to the world.

Domain Name

A domain name is the beginning of good SEO (search engine optimization). Invest time in its inception.

Basic Guidelines

1. Avoid using misspelled words, numbers, and hyphens. The misspelling of words in a domain name is sometimes used for branding or because the correct spelled word was already taken. Although it might be clever and fun to come up with alternative spellings (affiliatetracks.com becomes affil8trax.com) doing so makes ranking more difficult. It then becomes necessary to invest time and money into a branding campaign and detracting your focus from building your business.
2. Keep it short. Have you heard of "long-tail" domains? These are domain names that read like a sentence such as

howtogetthebestdomainnamesintheworld.com.The intended strategy here is that someone will enter a Google search on "how to get the best domain names in the world" and because the domain name is an exact match of the search, it'll appear near the top of the results. Search engine algorithms are more demanding than that, however, the strategy can work in certain applications. For your best digital self, a much more people-friendly domain name is necessary. After all, no one is going to type out a sentence to visit your website.

3. Consider using your name as the domain name. What better way to represent your best digital self than naming your website after you? Naturally, the more common and phonetically spelled the name, the easier it'll be for people to find online. However, even if your name has a unique spelling, I'd recommend getting it registered. Your name will be on your business cards and newsletters and it's uniquely you.

4. Make it relevant. If you're an entrepreneur, then using your name is highly relevant. Alternatively, if you have set up an LLC or some other corporate structure, then register your company's name as the domain. For myself, I've registered both my name and company's name and I recommend you do the same. If you have not yet set up a company but are considering doing so, then search the name both as a company and domain name before coming to a decision. After all, you do not want to create an LLC named Awesome Networks to only find out later that awesomenetworks.com was already taken.

Service Providers

When seeking out service providers for your online presence avoid relying on "Top 10" lists. In most cases, these are created by people that have affiliate links to all 10 vendors on their list. They're not interested in providing real information but are simply after the commission. Instead, search out real customer feedback. When it comes to domain registrars and hosting providers, costs range greatly. For hosting providers, quality of service and technical support is vital so do not default to the lowest cost. For my recommendations please visit my site, EdKeener.com. I do use affiliate links but you're not going to get a long list of options and I only recommend services I use.

Uniformity

It's common practice for entrepreneurs to have a website, YouTube channel, Facebook page, a Google 'My Business' profile and so on. Be sure, as much as the various platforms will allow, that visually there's a cohesiveness throughout these properties. Avoid giving mixed messages regarding your services. For example, if you're a professional wedding photographer, then avoid the temptation of having landscapes photos in your Instagram account.

CMS (Content Management System)

When it comes to presenting your online masterpiece there's no shortage of options. I'm a fan of WordPress. WordPress can be as simple or complex as you need it to be. For beginners, it provides an easy to use means of implementing a countless supply of themes and plugins. There are now several high-quality page builders available to WordPress users which gives more flexibility than traditional themes but without the need of knowing code. For sites, I develop I use Elegant Theme's Divi Builder. It's powerful enough to do what's needed and yet simple enough that when the time comes to hand over the reins to the site owner, I can teach them how to maintain and post to their site.

There is one constant in the tech world - it is always changing. The world trend of connecting to the Internet through mobile devices continues to rise. While I endorse the use of WordPress, I would be remiss not to mention the utilization of AMP (Accelerated Mobile Pages) and PWA (Progressive Web Apps).

AMP was developed by Google to provide content very quickly to mobile users. It is primarily used for articles and static content however it can be used to develop an entire website. When implemented a lot of the content is housed on Googles servers and information to mobile visitors is presented much faster than more traditional websites.

PWA is an attempt to blend a traditional website with the functionality of a mobile app. This hybrid allows a mobile visitor to have an icon appear on their mobile phone and this acts as a shortcut to your site. It also allows the site owner to send out push notifications. However, using a PWA as the sole CMS does not necessarily grant super-speed content delivery. The forward-thinking entrepreneur will use PWA as a shell around AMP content. In this way, you'll get the functionality of PWA and the speed advantages of AMP.

When creating your corner of the Internet, there's a lot of factors to consider. While I've provided some insights here it is not meant to be comprehensive. I enjoy assisting entrepreneurs in bringing their uniqueness alive online. Please feel free to contact me through my website.

***

To contact Ed:

https://edkeener.com.

Ryan Renick

Ryan Renick is a twenty-two-year-old business owner and entrepreneur from Plano, Texas. Recently he graduated from The University of Arizona, where he launched his CBD business Whole Body Hemp. Renick grew up around business development his entire life and has built a network of impressive relationships which he has utilized and linked together to not only lead to the success of others but as well as his own. His motivation to help others is the very foundation of which his company Whole Body Hemp is built on. He knows that so many people in the world face problems that they cannot face on their own just as he has been through and strives to help those in need in any way possible that he can. Aside from his own business, Renick consults with other entrepreneurs who aspire to build health and wellness companies. He is a creative individual who has all of the right parts to take an idea and make it a reality and build a successful company. There is no doubt that this young motivated entrepreneur will have tremendous success for years to come.

Cracking the Code to Being Rich

By Ryan Renick

Successful people do not all have the same story, but they do have a similar way of how they go about their life in order to achieve their level of success in one way or another. Throughout my life, I have met more successful people than I can count. They have each taught me the essential ways of life that I have taken and applied which have helped lead me to my own successes. Throughout this book, you have read the amazing stories of numerous entrepreneurs from significantly different walks of life, but I can tell you that the way each of them got there is not all that different. The first thing that is similar about each successful individual's story is exactly that…they all have a story which is the foundation for their success. A story is the essence of a person or a company's success because it is what sets them apart. A sort of background that leads them to their passions or their "reason" for action. Many people attempt to get into a space of a particular industry without any relation to it, and this ends up typically as a failure.

Take into consideration my personal story of how I got involved in the CBD industry. I did not just one day decide that I was going to begin working in the cannabis industry. There were multiple factors and stages of my life that lead me to that. My story of wanting to help others live a healthy life starts back when I was a thirteen-year-old boy in the Fall of my eighth-grade year. It was that year that my father was diagnosed with Leukemia, of which he was 87% infected and was told he would only live for five more years. This was a lot to digest as a young teenager, but was the part of my life that shaped me into who I am today. Through the following several years while I was in high school, my father went through multiple rounds of chemotherapy and underwent a triple-bypass open heart surgery simultaneously. At this time, before going into my Junior year of high school, I had been hit by a drunk driver. I nearly lost my life but only suffered a major concussion, as well an injury to my back. This was just one of the 5 concussions I suffered in high school, four of the others from playing Texas high school football. When my father underwent open heart surgery, for two weeks I would go from two-a-days to the hospital to visit him. At this time, his weight had dropped from 240 pounds to 180 pounds and watched him fight for his life. Meanwhile, I took care of my mom who would cry many nights while my father was at the hospital as I was at home trying my best to be the man of the house. Despite all signs pointing in the worst directions, my father never gave up and prevailed through this hard time when the odds were stacked against him. He is alive today doing very well and continues to do treatment frequently. Over the years, many of his colleagues sent him samples of CBD products to try while he was struggling with his leukemia and it proved to help him tremendously through his treatment.

Circling back to my own experience which led me to be introduced to CBD, was after my sophomore year of college. The injuries that I sustained in high school were catching up to me. My headaches from my concussions turned in to frequent migraines, I developed severe anxiety which grew into signs of depression, and the chronic pain from my injuries grew worse and worse. I was at a point where I thought I would have to deal with this for the rest of my life and have to resort to chemically saturated products to get me through my day to day life. I had obviously heard of and personally seen the results of CBD products, but was somewhat skeptical. However, I had nothing to lose and figured it was worth a shot. Since I made the decision to give CBD a chance, the results have changed my life forever. No longer do I go through my day with constant back and shoulder pain, and I can actually work out and be fit without suffering the pain from my past injuries. My headaches are nearly nonexistent, and my vocabulary and memory improved beyond what I could've ever imagined. I am remembering things I hadn't remembered for years as well as using words that I had never used before. I am significantly more awake throughout my day and more attentive to my surroundings. What I'm most thankful for though, is how much it has truly helped with my anxiety as a natural substitute for prescription medications that I personally refused to take.

CBD works best only if you are taking it consistently. Which brings me to the first essential key for an individual to be successful, consistency. Of course, there are several other factors that contribute to success but none of them will have the outcome you wish to attain unless you are consistent. You must make these factors habits in your everyday life, that way it is not a matter of *if you feel like doing it*, it comes down to *how* you get it done. With a habitual routine, these habits become natural. Consistency brings the balance of these factors of success to life if you apply yourself.

The first of these factors is that you must not make assumptions of people or situations. When you are facing a situation or meeting someone for the first time, it is to your benefit for you to go into that situation or relationship with an open mind. When you make assumptions, you are putting a cap on the endless possibilities that could be, because you are allowing them to be limited. Despite what you may know about similar situations or things you may have heard about that person, your initial interaction with them should be viewed with an open mind. When I say this, I mean that you do not know what you are capable of doing with this person or situation, and you never will unless you go into it with an open mind and explore the endless possibilities that could lead to the ultimate success that you so desire. Assumptions are associated with negativity, and the second you make them creates negativity within the situation or relationship. Instead of making assumptions, it is beneficial for individuals to ask questions directly or look at situations through different lenses to determine if the subject is beneficial for you. No one likes to waste time, which is a reason why people jump to conclusions. To be most efficient with your time, ask questions to develop a clear picture in order to recognize how to correctly utilize the situation or relationship, and if it will help you reach the level of success you are working towards.

The next concept, which is relative to not making assumptions, is saying "yes" to opportunities you are presented with. When you don't make assumptions, and allow opportunities to blossom by saying yes, you increase your chances of reaching the level of success you seek. You might embark on a journey you did not anticipate, in an industry you would have never expected to be in, but that is what is so special about saying yes. You will learn more about yourself than ever before, and realize that you have capabilities and knowledge in areas that you had no affiliation with prior. Saying "yes" also expands your network of contacts. Everyone has heard the saying, "It's not what you know, it's who you know", and people with expansive contacts didn't build their rolodex by saying "no" to opportunities. They said yes to as many people and situations as they could, and did everything in their power to make the most of that situation. There have been numerous times that I have had someone ask me if I could do something for them in relation to business, and more times than not I had no personal knowledge on how to carry out that task. Alternatively, I always knew someone that could do such task, or someone I knew, knew someone that could. Through connecting these people, I would learn how to handle the task at hand. In doing so, I became so knowledgeable in the subject, where I was qualified to aid anyone with the same need in the future. Saying "yes" to more opportunities overall will make you more prepared to take on whatever it may be that life throws at you.

 In relation to your network of people, one of the most essential concepts of reaching success is surrounding yourself with people who are smarter than you. Some people hold the belief that you should always be the smartest in the room. This can be true, but you do not just become the smartest person in whatever room you step into, there is much more to it than that. The people that you interact with the most and surround yourself with should be people that you are constantly learning from. When I was younger, I was constantly surrounded by individuals who were significantly older than me who were working with my father. I would always listen to what they would discuss and digest the knowledge that they were speaking so I could apply it later on in life. When I got into my twenties and started working in a career, I found myself working with a lot of individuals that were more than twice my age. Interestingly, I found it extremely easy to work with them from what I learned earlier on in my life. I noticed that a majority of the people in my corporate inner circle were extremely successful people that were much older than me and I would learn from them daily. You must listen and ask questions on concepts that are not clear to you, but when you find the right mix of successful people you are surrounding yourself with, you will find yourself achieving the same level of success or even more so.

The next factor is what establishes your credibility within your network for people to be able to trust you. This is the concept of committing to what you say, as so many people speak empty words. This means they might "talk the talk" but can't "walk the walk". Committing to what you say earns you the respect that you need to be a successful person. An essential quality of the most successful people in the world is how respected they are, and they did not earn that respect by lying their way to that status. Instead, they committed to their word and followed through with their commitments. Through committing to your word, you create the life you want because you must not only commit to your word to others, but you must commit to your word within yourself. Through doing this, you can manifest the life of your dreams. This is why one should never make assumptions, as I mentioned earlier. Making assumptions and committing to those assumptions leads to negativity in your life. This can lead to you manifesting negativity into your life, and implement a pattern of toxicity leading you further away from the success that you so wish to achieve. You must commit to your word without making an assumption to ensure a positive outcome. To commit to your word within yourself, you must keep yourself accountable with every other factor I have talked about thus far, and you must be consistent with your accountability for yourself. When you are consistent with keeping yourself accountable for committing to your word, you will achieve everything aspire to.

Through carrying out all of these concepts that attribute to success, nothing will reach its full potential unless you put everything you have into it. For you to understand this concept, you must realize that your potential will not be the same on every venture, you will have ones that you thrive with and one that you struggle with but when you apply yourself the best you can you will achieve the best outcomes that you can. I will say that if you make the other factors

I mentioned before of being consistent, not making assumptions, saying "yes", surrounding yourself with smarter people, and committing to your word, you will find that your potential will grow in every area you could possibly imagine. You must live your life to your full potential. You must continuously move forward and treat yourself to the full potential that you are capable of and take care of yourself the best you can, both physically and mentally. Practice these habits and it will become much easier to work at your full potential. Something that one must keep in mind when applying your full potential in everything is that you must not overstep your boundaries. Doing this can lead to yourself burning out and lead to an end result that seems as if you gave up at the end. When you utilize your full potential, you cannot question yourself asking, "Did I do everything I could have done?" because you know you did and there is no way for you to personally feel guilty.

Being a successful individual, you have to realize you are going to have critics and not everyone is going to agree with you. You have to be able to handle the heat and varying thoughts of others while not taking the criticism directly. Taking other's criticism directly is the ultimate form of egoism, and when people see that you have an ego, it is easy for others to take advantage of you and your ego because it is the ultimate weakness. You have to realize that you are not going to win every battle. Successful people have experienced more moments of failure than success. You must know that eventually, your methods will pay off. Again, it is just a matter of consistency. Taking other's criticism directly is taking responsibility for their actions. But if you follow the factor I mentioned before, you are not committed to their word, you are committed to your own. If you hold yourself responsible to your own actions and do not take the criticism of others directly as your own, then you will never find yourself questioning yourself, and know you did everything you could possibly do to your full potential.

Not everyone is going to have the same story. My hope is that after you have read this book of amazing success stories and the methods of how people reached the levels of success that they have, that you feel inspired. Remember that it all starts with consistency. Your success is dependent on you being consistent with applying everything you have learned about reaching the level of success that you desire. You must be open minded and not make assumptions to open the world of opportunity in order to reach that success. You should say "yes" and take advantage of as many opportunities to increase your chances of success. Surround yourself with people who are smarter than you, so that you are always learning and can become a product of their success. Commit to your word so you can become a respected individual of those you surround yourself with. Apply yourself with everything you have to get the best results out of everything you do. Lastly do not take the criticism of others directly, as you are only in charge of yourself, and if you don't take that criticism directly then you will never question your actions. The first step is finding your story and if you don't have one, then go make one and that will be your first step in cracking the code to being rich.

***

To Contact Ryan:
Website: Wholebodyhemp.net
Instagram: @Wholebodyhemp
Twitter: @WholeBodyHemp
Facebook: Whole Body Hemp
Email: wholebodyhempceo@gmail.com
Phone: (954)-261-8871
Address: 5048 Tennyson Pkwy. Suite 250, Plano, TX 75024

Afterword

Life and business is always a series of transitions… people, places, and things that shape who we are as individuals. Often, you never know that the next catalyst for improving your business and life is around the corner, in the next person you meet or the next book you read.

Jim Britt, Kevin Harrington and Joel Sauceda have spent decades influencing individuals and entrepreneurs with strategies to grow their business, developing the right mindset and mental toughness to thrive in today's business environment and to live a better life.

Allow all you have read in this book to create a new you, to reinvent yourself and your business model if required, because every business and life level requires a different you. It's your journey to craft.

Cracking the Rich Code is a series that offers much more than a book. It's a community of like-minded influencers from around the world. A global movement. Each chapter is like opening a surprise gift, that just may contain the one idea that changes everything for you. Watch for future releases and add them to your collection. If you know of anyone who would like to be considered as a co-author for a future volume, have them email our offices at support@jimbritt.com

The individual and combined works of Jim Britt, Kevin Harrington and Joel Sauceda have filled seminar rooms to maximum capacity and created a worldwide demand. If you get the opportunity to attend one of their live events, jump at the chance. You'll be glad you did.

If you are an entrepreneur and would like to get the details about becoming a coauthor in the next Cracking the Rich Code book in the series, contact Jim Britt at jimbritt@jimbritt.com.

To Schedule Jim Britt, Kevin Harrington or Joel Sauceda as a featured speaker at your next convention or special event, email: support@jimbritt.com

Master your moment as they become hours that become days.

Make it a great life!

Your legacy awaits.

STAY IN TOUCH WITH JIM, KEVIN AND JOEL

For daily strategies and insights from top entrepreneurs, join us at

THE RICH CODE CLUB

FREE members site.

www.TheRichCodeClub.com

www.ingramcontent.com/pod-product-compliance
Lightning Source LLC
Chambersburg PA
CBHW061206220326
41597CB00015BA/1535